inhabit**BRAND**

Enabling Brands For What's Next

ESMÉ ROTTSCHAFER

Popjunkie Culture Goods Inc.

Published by Popjunkie Culture Goods Inc.
ISBN: 978-1-0695933-0-6 (Paperback); 978-1-0695933-1-3 (eBook)

First edition

Book Cover and Illustrations by Tyler Serr

Print-on-demand paperbacks are printed in the country of purchase, bulk copies printed in Canada.

For more information: inhabitbrand.com

For those who are ready to inhabit Brand differently.

And, for everyone who helped and hand-held along the way.

CONTENTS

1. Brand Inheritance   3

introduction   5

what it means to inhabit   7

what is brand strategy?   9

a brief history of brand strategy   14

the inheritance problem   33

where purpose drifted   39

why brand strategy must change, now   44

2. Enabling Possibility   53

inheritance to inhabitance   55

era of possibility   58

enablement   67

what's shaping futures?   72

the changing shape of brand relationships   90

when brand becomes infrastructure   112

3. Inhabit Brand   119

building for what's next   121

new foundations   122

inhabiting brand   125

outcomes over vision   134

the brand operating idea   137

enabling possibility: in practice   142

the inhabit process   154

what this is for   163

4. Notes & References   165

tl;dr   167

doubts, pushbacks, & but-what-abouts   169

interludes & figures   179

references & reading   180

about the author   193

inhabit inhabit inhabit inhabit inhabit inhabit inhabit
inhabit inhabit inhabit inhabit inhabit inhabit inhabit
inhabit inhabit inhabit inhabit inhabit inhabit inhabit
inhabit inhabit inhabit inhabit inhabit inhabit inhabit
inhabit inhabit inhabit inhabit inhabit inhabit inhabit
inhabit inhabit inhabit inhabit inhabit inhabit inhabit
inhabit inhabit inhabit inhabit inhabit inhabit inhabit
inhabit inhabit inhabit inhabit inhabit inhabit inhabit
inhabit inhabit inhabit inhabit inhabit inhabit inhabit
inhabit inhabit inhabit inhabit inhabit inhabit inhabit
inhabit inhabit inhabit inhabit inhabit inhabit inhabit
inhabit inhabit inhabit inhabit inhabit inhabit inhabit
inhabit inhabit inhabit inhabit inhabit inhabit inhabit
inhabit inhabit inhabit inhabit inhabit inhabit inhabit
inhabit inhabit inhabit inhabit inhabit inhabit inhabit
inhabit inhabit inhabit inhabit inhabit inhabit inhabit
inhabit inhabit inhabit inhabit inhabit inhabit inhabit
inhabit inhabit inhabit inhabit inhabit inhabit inhabit
inhabit inhabit inhabit inhabit inhabit inhabit inhabit
inhabit inhabit inhabit inhabit inhabit inhabit inhabit
inhabit inhabit inhabit inhabit inhabit inhabit inhabit
inhabit inhabit inhabit inhabit inhabit inhabit inhabit
inhabit inhabit inhabit inhabit inhabit inhabit inhabit
inhabit inhabit inhabit inhabit inhabit inhabit inhabit
inhabit inhabit inhabit inhabit inhabit inhabit inhabit
inhabit inhabit inhabit inhabit inhabit inhabit inhabit

1

Brand Inheritance

introduction

I almost gave up on brand strategy.

I didn't stop believing in it. I stopped believing in what it had become—even though Brand remains vital to what companies need today.

Somewhere along the way, something broke. I've watched Brand get reduced to voice and tone decks, campaign platforms, and one-page frameworks that no one uses. Brand strategy became a deck, not a decision-making tool.

Brand Purpose was supposed to fix this—give companies a soul, a reason to exist beyond profit. And for a while, it seemed to work. But eventually, purpose became static, safe, and performative. It lacked stretch. It rarely showed up in business models, products, customer experiences, or ecosystems. It inspired belief, but it didn't enable meaning, action, or outcomes.

For many organizations, Brand has become a marketing asset—a Power-Point slide, stripped of meaning and function, stuck in outdated frameworks, and starved of real influence.

For two decades, I have helped companies strategically define and build brands across various categories, industries, and diverse business ambitions. I believed, and still feel, that Brand is one of the most powerful advantages a business can leverage. It builds markets, not just image or reputation. It anchors meaning inside systems and creates value dynamically. And still, I've watched too much potential get lost in the gap between intention and implementation.

What I have come to understand, painfully and clearly, is that existing brand strategy models are too shallow, stoic, and linear. Most organizations are not structured to enable brand development. Brand strategy is not well understood or valued. Fixing this requires leadership and discipline.

Brand strategy needs a new model built for the complexity of today, the systems we need to navigate, and the people we claim to serve.

The result is this book. *Inhabit Brand* embodies what brands must do now: inhabit the systems in which they operate. To stop floating on the surface of marketing and start living at the centre of how businesses function to create and exchange value.

In some ways, it's a love letter to the full potential of Brand—a reckoning with why we've failed to realise it and a new way forward to help brand strategy regain its role as business logic.

Inhabit Brand is not just another framework. It's an evolution of how we think about brands, rooted in systems thinking, futures, and business design. It builds on what came before, but pushes beyond them, toward something more meaningful, functional, and alive.

What follows is my attempt to reimagine what Brand can do—if we return it to full function: Brand as the logic for the integrated design of value within a business system.

If you've ever felt that brand strategy is both essential and impossibly hard to get taken seriously, or ever wondered what comes after brand purpose, or wished brand strategy had more traction inside the business, you're the intended reader.

It's written for people who understand the importance of Brand but feel stuck. For strategists, founders, CMOs, designers, and anyone else asking: "Why doesn't brand work the way it should?"

This book is my contribution to answering that question.

what it means to inhabit

I kept coming back to this word—*inhabit*. It felt right. Not passive. Not performative. Rooted. Alive. It captured how I think, how I work, and what I believe brand strategy is meant to do.

Inhabit reflects my approach to brands—as systems to be activated and enablers of futures. As opportunities to make something more possible—for the business, for the people it serves, and for the world it moves through.

When I think about the brands that feel most vital—the ones that unlock new value or feel culturally inevitable—they don't just occupy space. They respond to it. Shape it. Use it.

That's what I mean by *inhabit*.

It's not about "living your brand"—a phrase that feels theatrical. It's about bringing your brand into living systems.

The brands I've seen succeed don't just follow trends or meet consumer needs—they inhabit possibility. They seek the spaces between what is and what could be—and move into those spaces with intention. They don't wait to be relevant. They become essential by enabling something new.

To inhabit is to be fully present wherever your brand can create value. It's adaptive and generative. It requires fluency in systems and fidelity to meaning. It's about understanding how business works, how people live, how culture shifts, and designing your brand to move within those rhythms.

To truly inhabit a market is to understand its dynamics, but also to help others shape it, evolve it, and build within it. The best brands don't just disrupt—they *enable*. They don't just scale—they *support*.

That's the invitation of this book: to reimagine Brand as a strategic system that inhabits its environment—and makes things possible.

Not just brands that show up in the market, but brands that show up *for* the market. Brands that don't simply inhabit space, but expand what's possible within it.

This kind of inhabiting requires a different approach to brand strategy—one rooted in systems, built for complexity, and designed to anticipate what's next.

It's how brands reach their full potential.
And it's why I love this discipline so much.

what is brand strategy?

Brand strategy is one of the most misunderstood disciplines in business. It's foundational, yet often treated as optional—frequently overlooked or misused. Despite its importance, we rarely talk about it with the precision or depth it deserves. And that starts with understanding the history of brand strategy—both in theory and in practice.

Brands have existed for centuries—as trademarks, symbols of quality, ways to build trust, and stand out. That was strategy, even if it wasn't called that. But *brand strategy* as a formal discipline emerged much later: first in the 1960s and 1970s, as management consultants introduced strategic planning and agencies formalized account planning. Then, codified academically in the 1970s-1990s through the work of Aaker, Keller, and others.

What's striking is that, even then, the best thinking recognized Brand as more than a marketing asset. It was a long-term business asset requiring deliberate, coherent design. Somewhere along the way, we lost that functionality.

This chapter isn't meant to be a crash course or a textbook. I'm not here to rehash Brand 101 or convince the most hardened skeptics. If you've picked up this book, I assume you already think Brand matters—and you want to unlock its full potential.

But to move forward, we need a shared understanding of what we mean when we refer to "brand strategy." Not just what it includes, but what it *does* (and what it needs to evolve).

So let's start with the definition. And then move beyond it.

What Brand Strategy Is—and Isn't

We tend to define it by its models, frameworks and applications or by confusing it with things that aren't brand strategy at all.

Some say brand strategy is your purpose, mission, or vision. Others define it as your positioning, promise, or USP. For some, it's the brand framework or a set of identity guidelines. And let's be honest—plenty of agencies still use "brand strategy'" as a catch-all for campaign or comms planning.

We talk about "brands" all the time—but rarely "brand strategy." That's because Brand has become shorthand for an asset: a logo, a name, a noun. Something to see, buy, or like.

But brand strategy is a verb set. It's about design, direction, and decision-making. And that's part of the problem: we've become fluent in speaking about Brand as a surface, not as a system. Until we restore the strategy behind Brand, we'll keep confusing expression for intent, and surface for structure.

We need to reunite brand as the thing people experience and brand as the strategic system behind it.

Brand Economics

Brand has always been business strategy. I've often referred to Brand as an "economic tool" to emphasize that it's meant to guide value creation—as a system that translates organisational capability into more capacity for growth.

And yet, we rarely talk about brands in economic terms beyond equity. We track awareness, health, and sentiment. We overlook how Brand reduces friction, enables scale, creates stability, fuels innovation, or expands business capacity.

This book's aim isn't to make the case for the value of Brand—there's plenty of literature that already does. But it's worth noting that Interbrand's annual *Best Global Brands* report consistently highlights the connection between Brand and business valuation, pricing power, and share price. They've also found that companies are inaccurately valued due to the misunderstanding of one key asset: *Brand*. In my experience, too, brands are critically under-leveraged as a source of value creation.

If we treated Brand as an economic system—rather than a storytelling or identity layer—we might finally build brands that don't just signal value, but are fully leveraged to create it.

Brand strategy isn't a message. It's not a logo. And it's definitely not a vibe. It's the operating system for what your business is trying to do in the world—and how it will do it.

Or at least, it *should* be.

In reality, brand strategy has been flattened. Reduced to campaign language, voice and tone slides, or half-hearted "why we exist" statements on corporate websites. Worse, it's often mistaken for planning: a sequence of outputs rather than a system of principles anchored in a strategic idea.

Real brand strategy has weight. It directs not only how a brand looks and speaks—but how it *works*. It should influence everything the brand is and does.

And by *everything*, I mean everything.

It should be an organizing idea—a strategic structure, a system that scales and adapts. Something a company inhabits, not a collection of disconnected efforts wrapped in Helvetica and hex codes.

There's no shortage of definitions of brand strategy. Many respected voices have shaped the field, and while their definitions differ in focus and phrasing, they orbit the same core themes.

David Aaker aligned with Keller, called it "a strategic process that creates a clear direction for the brand by determining its vision, strategy, and value proposition."

Trout and Ries defined positioning as "the act of defining and defending a unique position in the mind of the customer, relative to competition."

Philip Kotler defined it more broadly (if somewhat problematically) as "a long-term plan for developing a successful brand to achieve specific goals."

Interbrand calls brand strategy "the framework that ensures business decisions are made to optimize the relationship between an organization and its stakeholders."

Marty Neumeier described it as "the discipline of guiding the orchestration of all brand assets to build meaning."

Each definition tells us something essential. And together, they consistently speak to:

- Value creation

- Business decision-making

- Coherence and integration

- Distinctiveness and relevance

- Long-term orientation

- Holistic design

- Stakeholder alignment

First Principles
When you strip away the language, the models, the metaphors— what remains are two fundamental forces: **Meaning and Function.**

Meaning: How the brand creates personal, cultural, and emotional significance—the symbolic and relational value that drives human connection and decision-making.

Function: How the brand operationalizes meaning into practical value—through systems, products, experiences, and other tangible outcomes.

Meaning without function = just image.
Function without meaning = just utility.

Brand strategy must be the integration of both—across the full business system, from internal operations to the ecosystems it participates in.

A Definition for Complexity
With this in mind, the definition I use captures the interdependencies at the heart of modern brand building and it grounds Brand in providing a strategic structure within a dynamic context.

> **Brand strategy is the deliberate design of how an entity creates, delivers, and captures value by integrating meaning and function within systems, and across people, and contexts of exchange.**

It acknowledges that brands don't operate in isolation—they're shaped by people, enabled (or constrained) by systems, and must perform within constantly shifting environments. Instead, it holds space for identity, messaging, experience, innovation, business models, and behaviour—without being reduced to any one of them.

And most critically, it defines Brand as a system—adaptive, embedded, interconnected, and built to operate in complexity.

Next, we'll trace the evolution of brand strategy over time—the beliefs, ideas, and frameworks that shaped where the discipline has been, and how it operates today. Because, to understand why brand strategy must evolve—and what it must evolve into—we have to understand what we've inherited.

a brief history of brand strategy

When I first entered the field, I didn't know what to expect. I was new, naive, and just starting to learn the language of strategy. It didn't take long to realize that the language itself was part of the problem.

Everyone used strategy words interchangeably, all muddled together— positioning, promise, mission, USP, one word equity, value proposition—but each came from a different moment in time, shaped by distinct strategic needs.

I learned to work within the frameworks of the time, which in the early 2000s, were shaped mostly by CPG playbooks. These frameworks weren't empty. They were structured, familiar, and designed to create consistency across marketing assets and product teams. Brand strategy existed to serve the brand's identity and product point of difference. The job was to align messaging with tone, packaging with identity, and campaigns with a promise.

It was the era of integrated marketing communications at scale—what some called the "matching luggage" or "360" approach to campaign branding and creative planning. Brand strategy served product, packaging and advertising. And in most organisations, that's where it stayed.

What I didn't realize then was that I had stepped into a field built on layers of accumulated logic. Every generation had added—sometimes new, sometimes just renamed—without retiring what had come before.

Positioning stacked on mission.
Promise layered onto one-word equity.
Purpose was added beside vision.
Platforms were added atop value propositions.

Over time, brand strategy became an inherited stack delivered through frameworks that most organisations adopted without questioning how the parts fit together, or whether they still held any value.

This chapter is about unpacking that stack.

Because those layers didn't appear by accident. Each era of brand strategy emerged for a reason—shaped by its business environment, media logic, or cultural moment.

Some ideas were breakthroughs. Others incremental shifts.
Some still hold value. Others are holding us back.

The summary timeline of brand eras that follows will help us understand what we've carried forward—what each era tried to solve, and how those decisions shaped the discipline we've inherited today.

Brand Mark Era
(Pre-20th century)

Strategic Belief: Branding is an identifier of ownership and origin and then as a signifier of product quality and trust.

Cultural & Business Context: Brands originated as literal marks of ownership—to identify origin, signify trust, and convey trade value in marketplaces. It was branding as identity and later verification. Brand wasn't a personality or position—it was a guarantee of origin and quality.

How it Manifested: In the 1870s, branding was a new commercial concept which corresponded with legal identity protection via trademark law. This solidified the brand mark as a proxy for trust and something to be protected and owned. Brands like Quaker Oats, Pears Soap, and Heinz rose to prominence not just for what they offered, but because their marks symbolized reliability, safety, and repeatability in an unpredictable and often dangerous market.

The era emerged alongside the rise of industrialization and the early foundations of modern consumerism. Goods moved from producer to market with limited scale or competition. As production scaled, goods were no longer sold directly by known producers in familiar settings. Instead, consumers encountered products from unknown manufacturers on store shelves, in catalogues, or at growing urban markets.

The growth in logistics and transportation, as well as mass media, made brands more visible and enabled them to travel further which led to new needs for companies.

- Access: Industrial manufacturing and urban distribution made packaged goods widely available to mass consumers for the first time, including soap, flour, tea, and canned goods.

- Assurance: With no regulatory standards, food labelling, or safety frameworks, the marketplace was chaotic and unregulated. Consumers needed help making informed decisions.

Legacy: It planted the seed for Brand as economic and communication signals. And today, as brand trust erodes again, this era offers a powerful lesson: the original value of a brand wasn't how it spoke—it was what it guaranteed.

Core Contributions:

- Brands are a visual identifier of origin or ownership

- A concept rooted in trust and reputation

- Foundation laid for recognition, repeat purchase and loyalty

- Emergence of packaging as a brand medium

- Brand is a shortcut to the purchase decision-making process

But as markets grew more complex and competitive, simply marking the origin would no longer be enough to stand out or to sustain trust.

Brand Management Era
(1920-1940s)

Strategic Belief: Brands evolve from static identifier to managed commercial asset.

In the early 20th century, brands shifted from a passive mark of origin to a dynamic business asset—something that required oversight, investment, and strategic development. No longer just about labelling products, the goal was to create consistency, manage perception, and build preference in increasingly competitive markets.

Two major forces drove this shift:

- Market Maturation: As consumer markets developed and competition intensified, companies needed new ways to differentiate their products from those that were nearly identical. Grocery shelves placed rivals side by side, making packaging, perception, and placement key factors in purchase decisions. The expansion of mass retail, mass communication, and mass production coincided with this development.

- Organisational Scale: Mass production and growing product portfolios required systematic approaches to brand consistency. The challenge wasn't just how to produce—it was how to position and manage brands across complex companies.

Key Developments: The defining moment came in 1931 when Neil McElroy at Procter & Gamble wrote his now-famous memo proposing a "brand management" system for Camay soap. He argued that each brand should operate as its own business, with dedicated resources to fully tap its potential. Critically, this shift in attention moved from product category to brand, allowing multiple brands to compete within the same category, each offering distinct functional benefits.

Companies like Lever Brothers, General Mills, and Campbell's soon followed suit, adopting similar structures that laid the organisational footprint for marketing and category share.

This period also marked the emergence of consumer research and advertising as strategic functions:

- Daniel Starch, an American psychologist, pioneered early market research in the 1920s. He developed methodologies to measure advertising effectiveness through door-to-door interviews.

- George Gallup introduced the theory of "aided recall" to measure the effectiveness of advertising during this period.

- Claude Hopkins wrote about 'scientific advertising.'

- Alfred Sloan of GM introduced market segmentation to the company.

Though still early, these developments signalled a growing understanding of the consumer as a variable, not just a buyer. The integration of market research with psychology, sociology, and anthropology would mature more fully in the post-war period, but the seeds were planted here.

How it Manifested: Mass media, such as radio, created new reach. Brands could now speak directly into people's homes, and agencies responded by crafting slogans, jingles, and mnemonic devices to build brand recall. Strategy centred on memorability and product benefit.

This era formalized the connection between business, brand, and advertising. It offers an essential reminder that deliberately managed brands reach their full potential: a brand is a business function—a strategy to create consumer choice.

Core Contributions:

- Introduction of brand management as critical to competitive advantage

- Development of brand-centric organisational structures

- Separation of brand from production management

- Foundation for brand planning and performance accountability

- Advrtising established itself as the dominant tool of brand-building

- Emergence of ad recall, mass media influence and market segmentation

However, as competition intensified and similar products flooded store shelves, managing brands for name recall would no longer be enough—they would also need to feel different to stand out.

Brand Image Era
(1950-1970s)

Strategic Belief: Brand advantage is shaped by perception through emotional meaning and image.

Cultural & Business Context: The post-war boom created a perfect storm for brand evolution. Mass production met mass media, and suddenly, consumers were faced with the task of choosing between dozens of similar products competing for their attention. The 50s changed how people wanted to be communicated with. Brands shifted from internal organisation to external perception. Supermarket shelves were full. TV ads were loud. Functional benefits were harder to defend. Shelf space was no longer the only battlefield—mental space became the prize. The new question became: How do we stand out when everyone is saying something similar?

Key Developments: This challenge gave rise to three d stinct but related strategic currents. The *Mad Men* era brought big contributions to brand strategy from consumer psychology, creative advertising, business consulting and media theory.

1.The Unique Selling Proposition (USP)
Pioneered by Rosser Reeves in the 1950s and 1960s, the USP emphasized a single, repeatable product claim: "Buy this brand for this reason." His core belief was that simple, singular messages repeated over and over again were the way to influence brand recall. He didn't believe that being clever, subtle, or entertaining worked (he was talking about attention scarcity long before it was named.)

2.Brand Image and the Rise of Emotional Meaning

Running in parallel was the growing belief that what people felt about a brand mattered as much as what they understood about it In 1955, marketing scholars Burleigh Gardner and Sidney Levy published "The Product and the Brand" in *Harvard Business Review*, effectively introducing brand image and brand personality (the intangible aura around products) into marketing thought. This development was influenced by the sight, sound, and motion of television, allowing brand imagery to reach into living rooms with unprecedented emotional power.

Advertising pioneers like David Ogilvy, Leo Burnett, and Bill Bernbach championed this thinking, rejecting hard-sell logic in favour of emotional resonance and human tone. Where Reeves saw consumers as rational actors, Bernbach believed people bought on emotion: "Facts are not enough. Advertising is persuasion, and persuasion is not a science, but an art." Volkswagen's "Think Small" exemplified this new humanism—it wasn't about what you said but how you said it. Incidentally, the debate over advertising as an art or a science began in this era.

The emergence of brand image represented a fundamental shift—brands could now cultivate emotional territory in consumers' minds. A brand's image became a mental model formed by the accumulation of associations. Mindshare, as a strategic concept, only crystallized in the late 1960s and early 1970s. This marked the beginning of the idea of branding as relevance and brands as media constructs – what you said, and how, was your brand.

3.Brand Positioning

In the 1970s, many Western economies were facing inflation, slow growth, and market saturation. TV advertising dominated but had become overcrowded and expensive. The broader business culture shifted from expansion to protection, and brand strategy followed suit. Michael Porter's work codified business defensibility, encompassing competitive advantage, barriers, and edge. The war metaphors stuck.

It was in this climate that positioning emerged. In *Positioning: The Battle for Your Mind* (1981), Al Ries and Jack Trout reframed brand strategy entirely, combining USP's functional claims and brand image's emotional tone into a battle for cognitive real estate. The goal was to own a single idea and defend it relentlessly. Volvo stood for safety; FedEx for overnight; 7UP for "Uncola." When Volvo softened its design language, people's perception of safety dropped. That was the power and rigidity of positioning.

How it Manifested: Marketers began using brand positioning statements internally, bringing welcome focus and discipline, but also entrenching one-dimensional differentiation in brand strategy. The strategy became about defending competitive turf, rather than understanding people, opening the door for brands to make expressive claims that outpaced their operational realities. Consequently, this widened the gap between what brands said and what they actually did.

This era was the golden age of one-word strategy and one-way communication. Brands weren't ecosystems or experiences yet—they were ideas to be hammered into memory. Consumers no longer just bought the product. They bought the "point of difference" or "key benefit" of the product. And strategy became a process of editing down, not building up.

Core Contributions:

- Strategy begins with focused product claims that anchor messaging (USP)

- Brands become symbolic and emotional identities shaped by tone, story, and design

- Strategy evolves into owning a distinct idea in the mind, relative to competitors

- Ad campaigns are the primary tool for building both image and position

- Brand strategy becomes about defending mental territory rather than serving evolving consumer needs

As brands expanded globally and operated across multiple markets and channels, owning a single idea would no longer be enough—they would need systematic ways to manage and express that idea consistently everywhere.

Brand Equity Era
(1980s-1990s)

Strategic Belief: Brand must be consistently expressed and financially valued to drive long-term business advantage.

Cultural Context: As the 1980s arrived, so did a new corporate and cultural reality. These decades were dominated by scale, visibility, and control. Globalization accelerated. Brands expanded across markets and categories. The culture itself leaned into spectacle—celebrity, excess, and extraction. Everything was big: big business, big media, big expectations. Excess was the aesthetic. Brands were expected to be omnipresent, polished, and powerful. It was the American Psycho era of brands. The 1980s and 1990s were about making sure that the idea looked, sounded, and behaved the same everywhere. Strategy became about systematization. Companies were operating across geographies, categories, and communication channels. They needed structure. This environment demanded systemization—codifying ideas visually, verbally, and financially.

In the 1970s, JWT's Stephen King developed planning tools for understanding brand equity and consumer perceptions, effectively blending research into creative brand strategy. King's writing (such as "What is a Brand?" 1973) foreshadowed the systematic approach to brand identity that emerged in the 1980s, developing influential tools related to understanding brand equity.

This was the era of brand consolidation and corporate identity. Executives and marketers began to view brands as long-term assets that carry equity explicitly, but they also needed to be managed efficiently.

Key Developments: The late 80s saw the emergence of Integrated Marketing Communications (IMC)—a planning discipline that aimed to align messaging across all touch-points. The brand should speak with a unified voice and maintain a consistent look across every channel. Consistency was the key to managing and growing brand equity.

This era professionalized brand strategy into a core component of business strategy. Two interrelated concepts dominated: Brand identity (the strategic articulation of what the brand stands for and how it is expressed) and Brand equity (the value accrued in a brand, in terms of consumer preference and financial worth).

Design consultancies like Landor, Pentagram, Wolff Olins, and Interbrand rose to prominence, building brand identity systems and brand architecture that could scale globally. By the late 1980s, Interbrand pioneered the idea that brands could be treated as financial assets on the balance sheet. Brand had finally gained economic language. The CFO started paying attention.

The most significant development was the recognition of brand equity as a measurable business asset. David Aaker positioned a brand as a set of assets—awareness, perceived quality, associations, and loyalty—that could drive long-term value. Kevin Lane Keller built on this concept with formalized strategic brand management, linking positioning to marketing programs and equity outcomes.

How it Manifested: Brand frameworks, identity systems, guidelines and brand books—thick binders shipped to offices around the world. Consistency wasn't just aesthetic, it was strategic. Identity became infrastructure. Frameworks like the brand key (Unilever), brand pyramid, brand house, and brand prism (Kapferer) originated from brand design firms, management consultancies, academics, and large CPG brands like Unilever. They gave teams a common language and structure.

Companies began articulating their brand strategy using standardized components, including positioning, values, personality, mission, vision, and brand promise. Mission and vision—one described what the company did, the other where it was headed—were borrowed from management consulting and integrated into brand frameworks.

The brand promise emerged as a way to summarize positioning in a single, ownable expression—often used internally to brief teams in sprawling organisations. It told you what the brand wanted to deliver. But it did represent, for the first time, a gesture toward the consumer—not just as a buyer, but as someone whose trust and loyalty mattered. The brand promise was a signal of this shift toward 'relationship'.

Limitations: This was less an era of brand imagination and more an era of institutional legitimacy and managerial logic. Brands became rigid, polished, and perfected—as manufactured and engineered as the products of the time (Griswold's crunch enhancing, non-nutritive cereal varnish, comes to mind.)

Brand strategy was delivered in frameworks, identity enforced in manuals, and values were laminated in the break room. Everything looked right—but too often, it lacked cultural depth. It was now something to be managed, measured and repeated, not just expressed.

Core Contributions:

- Brand identity systems codify expression across touchpoints

- Brand equity models link the brand to financial and strategic performance

- Brand frameworks emerged to structure internal articulation and planning

- IMC sought consistency across proliferating media channels

- Brand became a managed asset—institutionalized but distanced from culture

But as the internet emerged and consumer voices grew louder, this controlled, systematic approach to branding would soon face unprecedented disruption.

Identity Era
(1990s–2010)

Strategic Belief: Brands must adapt to digital transformation and become social entities.

Cultural & Business Context: The 2000s shattered the controlled brand environment of previous decades. The internet democratised media and social platforms enabled conversation. Together, 9/11 and early recession cycles created uncertainty. Brands faced media fragmentation, shortened attention spans, and the first wave of consumer control. Marketing shifted, media exploded, and culture cracked open. Brands were trying to evolve, but their strategies were not keeping pace. Traditional one-way communication was breaking down. But no new strategic centre had emerged to replace positioning and promise.

Key Developments: This wasn't an era of unified thinking—it was a pile-up of thinking about how brands needed to function. New ideas, new language, and new demands aimed at standing out, addressing fragmentation, and moving beyond the message and into culture.

- **Brand Storytelling** gained prominence as narrative became a differentiator across channels.

- **Challenger Brands** (*Eat Big Fish*, 1999) reframed the approach to competing against category leaders.

- *Emotional Branding* (Gobe, 2001) prioritized emotional appeal over functional benefits.

- *The Experience Economy* (Pine & Gilmore, 1999) positioned brands as creators of experiences.

- *Affinity: Beyond Branding* (Goldfarb & Aster, 2010) created the alignment between meaning and self with brand attraction.

- *Paradox of Choice* (Shwartz, 2004) emphasized brand simplicity as a response to choice overload and complexity.

- *Cultural Branding* (Holt, 2004) showed how brands become icons through myth and cultural markets.

- **Brand Archetypes** (*Hero and The Outlaw*, 2001) provided personality frameworks for brand character.

How it Manifested: Brands attempted to be more human, authentic, and interactive, primarily through advertising communications. CSR emerged but stayed siloed from Brand. Campaigns like Dove's "Real Beauty" proved that cultural relevance was achievable. Apple demonstrated that simplicity could be a strategic advantage.

Social media forced brands to learn how to be 'friends.' It was the decade when we tried to humanize brands—make them 'authentic,' 'real,' 'like a friend.' Mr. Clean got his own facebook page—he was popular with the ladies. Brand affinity reinforced attraction, while branch character supported social engagement. Brands were now supposed to interact, not just announce. But it wasn't yet behavioural—it was still stylistic. The language changed, but the systems hadn't caught up.

The image-led logic of previous eras began to crack under the weight of interaction. Brands could no longer rely on static identity or top-down messaging. Engagement was starting to matter and be measured. Social media was emerging. People could now talk back. Brands began to feel their edges.

Core Contributions:

- Recognized that media fragmentation required new approaches

- Introduced storytelling as a strategic tool

- Elevated experience and emotion as brand differentiators

- Began experimenting with cultural relevance and engagement

- Started humanizing brand language and interaction

Limitations: This era generated ideas without integration—proliferation created confusion rather than clarity. Brands were trying to be more than their products—to speak to values, aspirations, and shared experiences. But for all this energy, there was no new strategic centre. Just a growing sense that something had to change, while most innovations remained at the level of communication.

It was Brand's postmodern moment. Ideas coexisted, theories overlapped, and models often contradicted one another—each trying to fill a growing strategic gap. It was noisy, reactive, and full of ambition. But it laid the groundwork for what came next.

When brand purpose arrived, it felt like a breakthrough—a fundamental shift. It wasn't built from scratch, but it offered something the industry was hungry for: coherence, conviction, and a single organizing idea. After a decade of overlapping trends, ideas and tactical fragmentation, purpose promised to unify it all. And people grabbed on—hard.

Brand Purpose Era
(2010s–2020s)

Strategic Belief: A brand must exist for something bigger than profit—anchored in belief, values, and behaviour.

Cultural & Business Context: The Brand Purpose Era emerged at a time when people were searching for meaning and demanding more. Following the financial crisis of 2008 (and the Enron and WorldCom disasters), trust in institutions and governing boards was low, expectations of business were shifting, and brands were under increasing pressure to present themselves differently. Purpose became the dominant anchor for brand strategy to replace positioning. And it changed the primary question of brand strategy to "Why do we exist?"

Corporate behaviour and post-recession disillusionment drove demand for integrity and action. Meaningful consumption emerged as a macro-driver, shifting consumer expectations as ethical, sustainable, and identity-aligned choices became increasingly central to their purchasing decisions. It was about why you buy, not what you buy.

Digital transformation altered how people discovered, interacted with, and judged brands. Social media created new pressures for transparency, positioning brands as public actors and media entities.

Key Developments: This era introduced a new kind of brand citizenship—brands weren't just participating in culture, they were actively shaping it.

Simon Sinek's *"Start With Why"* (2009) gave Purpose a TED Talk glow-up. Suddenly, "why we exist" became the centrepiece of every brand presentation. Jim Stengel's *"Grow"* (2011) linked ideals to business performance. Mark Earls reframed brands as social actors, expanding the role from communication to contribution. Leo Burnett's Humankind model codified Purpose into robust planning tools, championing cultural fuel, behaviour change, and acts over ads.

Platform thinking—influenced by Big Tech—began to influence how brands thought about digital infrastructure. Brands began building their own channels and direct relationships, rather than relying solely on traditional media. Few became true platforms, but many built digital hubs, apps, and tools to foster engagement. Even when incomplete, this logic shaped ecosystem design.

A different kind of platform thinking also emerged within brand building itself—brand platform ideas, such as Coca-Cola's "Open Happiness," Dove's "Real Beauty," and Red Bull's "Gives You Wings," that could drive coherent brand building across touch-points and campaigns.

Behavioural economics gained mainstream traction, challenging classical decision-making models. Thinkers like Thaler and Sunstein (*Nudge*), Dan Ariely, and Daniel Kahneman reframed consumer behaviour as emotional, biased, and context-shaped rather than rational. These ideas influenced performance marketing, UX and measurement, giving rise to 'nudging' and brand activation.

How it Manifested: This wasn't a communications exercise—it was a strategic reframing. Brands began to operate as if they had a stake in the world, aligning with causes, taking cultural sides, and connecting to communities through shared beliefs and values.

Purpose moved upstream into boardrooms, reshaping internal narratives, employer brands, and recruitment strategies. It created expectations for organisational alignment. In the best cases, Purpose became a strategy for business behaviour, employee engagement and consumer value, though this required leadership that could reach across the entire company.

Lifestyle brands like Nike, Patagonia, and Lululemon became case studies in living Purpose through products, culture, and communities.

Meanwhile, brands were learning to be digital, agile, and always-on. Technology began to dominate advertising logic through behavioural economics, CRM pipelines, and programmatic delivery in digital environments where every click could be baited, tracked and optimised.

Design thinking and customer experience became core ideas. The rise of CXD brought a hyper-focus on frictionless design, and usability, although most customer journeys were designed for conversion, not meaning. While user experience design matured, brand experience remained underdeveloped, despite successful examples like Starbucks, Disney, and Lego.

While brand purpose was gaining traction, so too was the value proposition. It became dominant in startup thinking—especially with Business Model Canvas and Lean methodology. As startups scaled through DTC and SaaS platforms, brand strategy was often replaced with a single-minded focus on value propositions: what problem are we solving, for whom, and why are we better at it? This approach contributed to the marginalization of the brand in digital-first companies. We were back to the USP—albeit a more sophisticated one.

This digital-first thinking led to "blanding"—hyper-minimalist, lookalike brands shaped by digital design systems and DTC aesthetics. As companies optimised for seamless user experience and platform scalability, branding became uniform: featuring soft tones, sans-serif logos, geometric icons, and Instagram-like mimicry. It was branding designed to perform across digital interfaces, but often lacked meaning, distinction, or depth. It reflected the era's tension: purpose demanded meaning, while systems rewarded frictionless sameness.

Behaviour became the strategic thrust but split into two directions. For brand purpose, behaviour was meaningful—signalling values and aligning belief with action. For digital marketing, behaviour became trans-actional—tracked, nudged, clicked, optimised. As ad platforms matured and attribution became cemented, performance marketing became easier to justify than brand work. Brands drifted toward broad ideals while marketing chased behavioural extraction. In this gap, brand and performance began to pull apart.

Core Contributions:

- Used purpose as a strategic container for meaning, identity, and action

- Elevated brand strategy to organisational behaviour, internal alignment

- Added contribution—not just differentiation—as a new strategic axis

- Elevated brand's role as a cultural and moral actor within society

Limitations: As Purpose matured, its edge began to dull. What started as a philosophical shift often became marketing theatre—the gap between what was said and what was done created backlash. Purpose was too frequently treated as a one-dimensional tool—used to signal virtue rather than build systems. It appeared in hero videos, while the rest of the business ran on clicks and code.

Again, meaning and function were at odds and Brand was stuck between them.

loveMARKS

In the twilight of the Brand Image era, Saatchi & Saatchi CEO Kevin Roberts introduced Lovemarks. This concept promised to transcend branding by building "loyalty beyond reason" through mystery, sensuality, and intimacy.

I worked at Saatchi when it launched. I read the book. I met Kevin. And yes, I fell for it.

Lovemarks arrived at a moment when traditional advertising was starting to feel tired and product differentiation was eroding. Categories were maturing, and companies needed to retain their customers. It offered a bold response: brands don't just need to be chosen–they need to be loved. Emotional storytelling became the tool. Love became the goal.

It was ambitious. Aspirational. And in hindsight...maybe just a little egotistical.

The problem? Lovemarks was rooted in the belief that love could be engineered through messaging, not behaviour. It asked for devotion without necessarily earning it. It imagined that if you just dialled up emotion, people would feel something more profound. But love doesn't work that way, not in life and not in branding. What Lovemarks actually delivered was a fantasy.

Still, Lovemarks left a lasting mark. It opened the door for emotion to be taken seriously in brand-building. It helped shift the focus toward brand affinity and the value of relationships. And while it overpromised, it captured something essential about the era: a desire for brands to matter more–to inspire, to connect, to mean something.

That desire didn't go away. But the methods would need to evolve.

The Brand Eras Timeline (*Fig. 1*)

Brandmark (Pre-1900–1920s)	Identifier of origin and quality	Trademark law, packaged goods, mass distribution	Visual marks as verification
Brand Management (1930–1950s)	Managed commercial asset	P&G brand management system, early consumer research	Organizational structures, category competition
Brand Image (1950–1970s)	Emotional differentiator	USP, Brand Image theory, Positioning	Mental territory, competitive framing
Brand Equity (1980–1990s)	Consistent, valuable asset	Identity systems, brand equity measurement, Integrated Marketing Communications (IMC)	Frameworks, guidelines, global consistency, financial value
Brand Identity (1990–2010s)	Social, cultural entity	Media fragmentation, storytelling, experience economy	Cultural and lifestyle relevance and engagement
Brand Purpose (2010–2020s)	Values-driven actor	Purpose as organizing principle, behavioural economics	Why companies exist beyond profit

the inheritance problem

Brand strategy began as a clear, contained discipline. Its early role was tightly bound to industrial era commercial growth, with a direct line between what a product promised and how it performed. Over time, that clarity eroded. With each era, the discipline took on more—expanding from identity to image, experience, culture, and purpose—yet its structures remained largely unchanged.

This widening scope created gaps: Less connection to business value. Less integration with operating systems and technology. And, less alignment between meaning and function.

Digital transformation accelerated the separation. As advertising became faster, data-driven, and algorithmic, brand strategy often stayed in frameworks built for slower, linear contexts. Historically, brand, markets and media moved together; now they were moving apart. The result was a discipline carrying more weight with less integration—often confined to marketing rather than embedded within the business.

To understand this detachment, we need to trace the discipline's evolution—not just by its surface changes, but by the underlying forces and contradictions that shaped it.

How We Got Here

By tracing Brand's historical trajectory, looking beneath the surface timeline of changing ideologies and contexts, we can see recurring patterns that reveal how Brand grew and why it faltered.

Each era emerged for good reason. Each solved real problems as the meaning and function of Brand matured. But each also carried forward unresolved tensions that ultimately set limits. By mapping these structurally, we can extract the imperatives that will guide the next era.

The Core Thread: Trust and Choice in Complexity
Across every era—from brand marks to purpose—one role has remained constant: helping people choose in contexts of complexity. Whether as a mark of origin, a symbol of belonging, or a promise of delivery, Brand has always served as a mechanism for decision-making.

The question isn't whether this role will continue, but how it needs to adapt to increasingly fragmented, distributed, and fast-moving environments.

The Strategic Arc
Brand is as much a business strategy as it is a cultural artifact. Its evolution reveals an expanding arc:

- Shortcut to product and category decisions

- Business asset and management system

- Expression of identity and cultural belonging

- System of behaviour and moral position

Brand communicated trust and choice through evolving mechanisms: identity, image, consistency, experience, belief, and behaviour. These cycles show how meaning and function continually stretched what Brand was expected to carry as markets matured, competition increased, and technology reshaped distribution and communication.

The Meta-Shifts Restructuring Everything
Beneath ideology and frameworks, larger systemic shifts pushed Brand away from static models and toward dynamic ones.

> *From Signal to System*: Brand began as a signal of origin and quality, became a container for emotion and culture, and evolved into a carrier of values and moral positions. What started as communication about products became orches-

trated experience, then partial attempts and behavioural follow-through.

From Ownership to Access: Brand shifted from what companies owned to what they could connect people to. Digital technology transferred control to consumers—who could research, compare, share, and opt out—forcing brands to earn attention rather than buy it.

From Product to Existence: Brand moved from distinctiveness and recognition into emotional resonance and cultural substance. Eventually it became about the very *existence* of the organisation—where behaviour and evidence determine credibility.

Together, these shifts stretched Brand's remit further than its inherited structures could support—leaving behind the fault lines we carry today.

The Contradictions That Accumulated

Each era left behind unresolved contradictions that compounded over time:

- **Meaning vs. Function** – Brands projecting meaning without operational depth; others delivering functionality without relevance.

- **Strategic Ambition vs. Scope** – Aspirations outpacing scope, eroding both meaning and function.

- **Expression vs. Experience** – Messaging rarely matching behaviour; experience optimized for conversion, not coherence.

- **Control vs. Participation** – Pursuing co-creation while clinging to control.

- **Brand vs. Tech** – Treating brand as expression and tech as utility, creating misalignment and missed opportunities.

These are symptoms of a discipline that expanded without a systems lens on brand.

Tethered to Marketing and Pulled Apart
Even as Brand's scope expanded, its foothold remained inside marketing. Without a foundation in business logic, strategy stalled—misunderstood, marginalized, or mistaken for something else.

The result was a widening split between brand strategy and the systems now driving marketing decision making. As marketing became algorithmic, behavioural, and performance-driven, strategy stayed anchored in static frameworks. What emerged wasn't just a philosophical divide but an operational one: one agenda pushing for values and meaning, the other optimised for attribution and conversion.

This left brand strategy conceptually rich but operationally vulnerable.

Design Imperatives for the Next Era
If the discipline is to evolve, certain conditions must be treated as non-negotiable. These aren't solutions in themselves but directional imperatives—design principles for the next evolution.

1. **Integrate meaning and function.** Resolve the split structurally, not sequentially.

2. **Design the brand as an adaptive infrastructure.** A system for value creation that maintains coherence through change.

3. **Shift from marketing to mechanism.** Strategy must coherently define how the brand works, not just how it communicates.

4. **Design for distributed reality.** Accept that meaning emerges across networks and design for participation.

5. **Embed strategy inside business logic.** Brand is not downstream from business; it is business logic.

6. **Resolve time horizon conflicts.** Prove value across multiple horizons, not just short-term gains.

7. **Reductive simplicity to expansive coherence.** Systems need

ideas that are singular in concept but generative in operation.

Together, these imperatives outline the conditions Brand must inhabit to remain structurally relevant.

The Weight of Inheritance

It's not about layering on another framework. It's about facing what the discipline has become. A brand is more than a communication tool—it's a shared model for interpreting value, making choices, and orienting in complexity.

Across its expansions, Brand solved real problems but accumulated unresolved gaps: meaning without function, ambition without capacity, expression without alignment. Over time, these compounded until brand could no longer carry the weight or keep pace with its environment.

This is the inheritance: a discipline rendered inert—analogue in many ways—struggling to operate in a digitalized, distributed world with more variables, ambiguity, and interdependence than ever before.

The clearest expression of this breakdown came in the rise of Brand Purpose—an era that promised to reconnect meaning and function but instead exposed how disconnected and vulnerable brand strategy had become.

yesterday's SOLUTIONS

In systems thinking, yesterday's solutions often become tomorrow's problems. The structures we build to solve one set of challenges create conditions for the next. Brand strategy is no exception.

Many of the frameworks that shaped the last several decades were effective in their time. They worked in stable markets, slower media cycles, and with customers whose choices were shaped by broadcast channels, linear brand narratives and categories.

But the same structures that once created clarity now often constrain adaptability.

This is what happens when the mental model stays fixed while the environment changes. In the iceberg model, we might say that most brand activity lives at the "visible event" level–campaigns, launches, new taglines–while the underlying patterns, structures, and mental models go unexamined. Without shifting what's beneath the surface, surface-level changes rarely hold.

The next era demands a different starting point. Brands need wholism–the ability to integrate meaning and function–because in complex systems, neither can sustain without the other. They need structural coherence that can flex with shifting contexts, avoiding the fragility that comes from designing only for current conditions. And brands need to work with, not against, the feedback loops that shape how they're actually experienced.

When we fail to see the system, we end up reinforcing the very problems we meant to solve: purpose statements that float above operations, experiences that don't match expression, campaigns that erode trust instead of building it. In complex environments, the real leverage is in redesigning the structures that generate those outcomes.

The real work now is to deepen our capacity to see the whole, to listen for what wants to emerge, and to design with consequences in mind. The point is not to perfect a system, but to keep shaping one that can learn – with us, through us, and beyond us.

where purpose drifted

With institutional trust collapsing and consumer values rising, the market was primed for a shift: buyers wanted to buy into brands, not just buy an image.

Brand purpose was supposed to connect meaning to function. But it rarely did. What began as a strategic reaction to brand superficiality eventually collapsed into abstraction—drifting away from the product, the customer, and, critically, reality.

The Ladder Logic Shifted
In the past, even transactional categories knew how to ladder benefits. A toothpaste brand might start with clean teeth but climb to confidence, attraction, or gut health. It connected product value to deeper human benefits.

As purpose took hold, the ladder reversed. Instead of building meaning from the product, many brands began assigning purpose at the organisational level. The result? A company selling deodorant claimed to dismantle toxic masculinity. A beverage brand became a platform for female empowerment. The leap was often too far—and too forced.

This shift left a vacuum in brand architecture. Companies no longer knew how to legitimately connect purpose to product or how to harness capabilities credibly against purpose. They struggled to balance belief with distinctiveness, long-term equity with short-term performance. Purpose may have added intent—but it didn't solve for the pressure to differentiate, convert, and sell.

The Purpose-Performance Divide
The say-do gap was real, but a deeper structural fracture had emerged:

brand strategy was losing even its traditional foothold in marketing as attention and investment were being diverted to short-termism and performance optimisation.

Purpose, framed as brand-building, operated in isolation from campaign cycles, media plans, or measurement. Meanwhile, performance marketing evolved in the opposite direction: hyper-targeted, cookie-dependent, optimisation-led—and almost entirely detached from brand meaning.

Ad spend still dictated how brands showed up, but media plans and creative briefs had to serve contradictory goals: reinforce purpose or drive performance. In practice, this meant toggling between "We believe…" messaging and "Buy now" offers—each undermining the other due to lack of interconnection.

Messaging became weirdly binary. Ads were either overly sincere or hyper-promotional. Neither approach built sustainable value. Brand affinity eroded. Messaging blurred. Branding became blanding.

And consumers noticed.
Ad-blocking rose.
Media effectiveness dropped.
Trust in advertising hit historic lows.

The machinery of modern marketing was actively cancelling out the consumer attraction that purpose was supposed to restore and the audience priming that brand-building was supposed to create.

When Purpose Became Moral Script
The deeper problem was structural: purpose was used as the strategy, not as a component of it.

Purpose originally meant clarification of intent—the why that defines existence. It didn't have to be moral. But over time, purpose was mistaken for virtue. Belief overtook the operational clarity it was meant to inform. Brands tried to align with consumer values without reshaping the products, policies, or systems that would make those values real.

As brand meaning expert Dr. Martina Olbert explains: "People are not buying your why. They're buying their own why." Purpose didn't fail because of expression—it failed because of structure. Purpose is internal: a guiding intent. Meaning is external: the value people receive. That confusion explains why so many brands sound like they're talking to themselves. They optimised for conviction—but lost connection.

Purpose, ironically, became another version of the brand talking about itself—just in more virtuous language.

Not every brand should save the world. But every brand should answer: What do we care about? And how do we show up accordingly—in a way people value?

The Critical Flaw in Purpose
Here's a core issue: Simon Sinek (like him or not) laid out the sequence—Why, How, What. But the industry obsessed over "Why" and jumped straight to "What." The "How"—the strategic mechanism that translates purpose into achieving vision—got skipped.

Purpose was the strategic intent. But companies used it as the "Why" and the "How"—expecting it to carry the weight of mission and positioning.

This created a breakdown. Purpose offered new language at a time when Brand was feeling empty. It created the impression of clarity—without doing the operational work to support it.

Because "purpose" sounded like action, it was often mistaken for a solution. It provided direction—without a roadmap.

Inside companies, this created a stall. Leadership declared purpose. Systems didn't change. Because purpose wasn't tied to measurement models, it became easy to ignore—or misuse.

The result diminished brand strategy itself as a driver of business value.

Structural Fatigue
When purpose was stretched across platforms, technologies, and ecosystems, it broke.

The outcome wasn't just consumer fatigue—it was friction. Teams struggled to reconcile belief with performance. Agencies couldn't balance conviction with conversion. Brand platform ideas couldn't compensate.

The purpose-performance gap became obvious and unsustainable. Trust suffered.

Even brand leaders began acknowledging it. Unilever CEO, Hein Schumacher publicly cautioned against "force-fitting" purpose where it doesn't make operational sense. A subtle but telling admission: belief alone can't carry the weight of strategy.

What Was Lost
When brands conflated purpose with moral performance, they lost something essential: texture, play, creativity, and humanity. They stopped being curious, overly sure of their own values, replacing wit with worthiness. Brands stopped taking risks. Even conviction started to feel unsafe.

The industry became, ironically, less meaningful.

The Limits Revealed
Purpose was the "Why." But we used it like the "How." We wrote inspiring statements filled with belief, intent, and narrative but skipped the bridge that could make them tangible, operational, and useful.

That "How" *is* strategy. How will we achieve our vision in a way that builds on our purpose?

The Purpose era elevated Brand within business and gave it new language beyond profit. But purpose was asked to carry too much. It promised to reconnect meaning and function yet often exposed just how fragile and disconnected brand strategy had become.

Purpose showed us the limits of Brand as inheritance. It revealed a discipline still tethered to old structures, unable to function across the systems that now define value. Which is why the next chapter isn't about purpose at all, but about strategy itself: why it must change now—before Brand becomes not just misunderstood, but structurally irrelevant.

tectonic TIMES

We talk a lot about acceleration. Fast-forward technologies. Generative tools. Exponential progress. Technology is evolving at breakneck speed.

But human experience doesn't move in lockstep with technology. Culture shifts unevenly, behaviour changes in waves, and meaning takes time to emerge. Together, they shift like tectonic plates—interconnected, uneven, full of friction.

Technological acceleration does not equal human readiness.

This tension introduces a temporal lag—a mismatch between what is possible and what is livable, between what can be built and what can be absorbed. Technology is outpacing institutions. Expectations are outpacing infrastructure. Potential is outpacing readiness.

Meanwhile, most economic and corporate systems remain wired for immediacy, prioritizing faster launches, growth, and returns. Efficiency as default. Optimisation as gospel.

But you can't hack your way to readiness. Acceleration without readiness doesn't create progress. It creates pressure. It drives short-term extraction instead of long-term evolution.

We can engineer conversion funnels and deploy tools that move faster, but we can't speed up a need or rush trust. We can't force a cultural shift into being.

If Brand is to operate as a system, it needs to be responsive to context, able to hold the tension between vision and reality, speed and sense-making.

What's possible, if activated with care, can make things more livable. It can ease the strain. Expand the frame. Reshape what once felt inaccessible into something more humane, more grounded, more inhabitable.

That's the point of futures and systems thinking. Not to accelerate—but to design the bridge between potential and reality.

why brand strategy must change, now

We're in a moment of strategic limbo. While many acknowledge that brand strategy needs to evolve, the responses reveal just how stuck we are in old paradigms. Some are doubling down on purpose, insisting the execution was flawed rather than the approach. Others are calling for brands to be more authentic, more human, more agile—without questioning the underlying frameworks. Meanwhile, industry conversations point to new requirements like participation or suggest tactical adjustments like better measurement, cleaner creative, more personalisation.

But these responses only capture part of what's actually happening. We're not facing a refinement problem—we're facing signals of a fundamental paradigm shift. The volatility, uncertainty, complexity, and ambiguity (VUCA) of the current moment aren't temporary disruptions to be weathered. They're permanent conditions that require entirely new approaches.

The evidence is everywhere, revealing how inadequate our inherited approaches have become, and why incremental change or tactical improvements won't be enough.

We're facing structural breakdown, not just strategic drift.

Systemic Breakdown
What we're seeing isn't just another branding cycle—it's a systemic breakdown across business, society, and culture. Institutions feel out of step. Systems feel brittle. People are burnt out. Trust in media, government, and corporations continues to fray.

In this atmosphere, it's no surprise that industries begin declaring things "dead".

This breakdown isn't just external—it's internal. Corporate leadership is regressing in tandem with political leadership. Using economic uncertainty as a pretext, companies are rolling back diversity initiatives, imposing return-to-office mandates, and abandoning sustainability commitments they once championed.

This regression reveals how easily proclaimed values get discarded under pressure—exposing the structural weakness of approaches that aren't operationally integrated.

Climate adaptation, AI ethics, employment redefinition, and global instability are pressing against institutional systems that were optimized for control, scale, and extraction, rather than ambiguity and emergence.

Requisite variety failure—when the challenges outside a system exceed the responses it can generate internally—is a common issue that many organisations face today. Brand strategy hasn't just fallen behind—it's become unviable. And unless it evolves into something more adaptive and systemic, it will continue to be misunderstood, misapplied, or devalued.

This misalignment doesn't reflect the death of Brand's role. It's reflects the failure of how we've tried to manage it. And the breakdown is the invitation to regenerate—not from a position of nostalgia but from one of necessity.

The Cost of Strategic Stagnation
While marketing has doubled down on performance and optimisation, the long-term structures that shape perception, preference, and participation have been systematically neglected. According to Interbrand, the world's top brands have collectively forfeited an estimated $3.5 trillion in value since 2000 due to under-leveraged or mismanaged brand strategy—and that's only what's visible. The deeper cost lies in what never got created: unrealized innovation, abandoned stretch, missed opportunities to become more useful, more embedded, more meaningful.

This represents a fundamental failure of strategic utility. Brand has been treated as a messaging layer when it should have been a structural driver. Despite growing recognition of its importance, brand strategy remains peripheral and structurally isolated from the business decisions that shape value (long-term and short-term).

This neglect has consequences. Financial stakeholders underestimate Brand's economic contribution. Interbrand found that 67% of S&P 500 companies may be inaccurately valued, in part because the influence of Brand on earnings and growth potential is misunderstood. Analysts know Brand matters—76% say it has a moderate to large impact on P/E (price-to-earnings) ratios—but 90% admit they don't have a deep understanding of brand strategy in the companies they cover.

This misalignment creates strategic stagnation, where surface updates are made, but the underlying mechanics of brand value creation go untouched. The brand becomes disjointed, unmoored from business logic, and ultimately underpowered.

In a world of AI, ambient trust systems, modular products, and identity-based commerce, brands must act as an interface between products and people, between systems and signals. If Brand can't show up in those spaces with depth and dimension, it simply won't show up at all.

The Environment has Changed—Radically
The term 'digital transformation' is no longer adequate to describe what we're experiencing now—a rewiring of value, interaction, and infrastructure that is deeper and more complex than digital alone. We have entered what many describe as the fourth industrial age, where AI, Web3, edge computing, participatory economics, and decentralized systems challenge our assumptions about scale, control, and ownership.

People aren't just buying differently—they're navigating the world differently. Algorithmic curation shapes reality. Emotional states are interpreted and responded to by intelligent systems. Brand experiences are now filtered through identity layers, wearable tech, and permission-based platforms. A person might never see your Brand, not because it isn't relevant, but because it isn't interoperable with their filters, preferences, or context.

It marks the end of broadcast-era brand logic. What matters now isn't reach—it's fit. Brand needs to be machine-readable, context-aware, and emotionally attuned. It needs to show up in the exact right tone, moment, and modality—not just to be seen, but to be selected, used, and trusted.

At the same time, the marketplace has fractured. Traditional platforms are giving way to micro-ecosystems of fandom, co-creation, and community-owned economics.Participation isn't just a marketing tactic—it's part of the operating model. Value is co-created in real-time, often with the very people strategies once tried to segment and target.

Brands need to act more like infrastructure and less like advertising, operating across emotional states, technology stacks, and cultural currents. It must be modular, ambient, and adaptive. The environment has changed. And Brand's role must change with it.

When Structure Contradicts Strategy
The inside of most organisations still treats Brand like a story, not a system. Brand strategy is built with the intent to influence far beyond marketing—across HR, product, experience, business model, and channels. Yet these companies remain structured for the opposite: linear workflows, siloed teams and departments, narrow scopes, and repeatable outputs.

This structural contradiction creates chronic misalignment. Brand strategy gets asked to inspire transformation while being resourced like a communication tool. Leadership frames it as a belief system while rarely investing in the systems part of the equation. Teams are tasked with managing company intent without access or resources to impact organisational systems. This creates a persistent disconnect between how a Brand wants to create value and how it actually shows up.

The knowledge gap compounds the problem. Internal brand understanding remains sparse across many companies. Few teams receive training in brand or strategy beyond surface elements like messaging and visual identity. Brand-building is often delegated entirely to marketing departments or external partners. Even the CMO role has become increasingly unstable, marginalized or absorbed into broader commercial titles focused on growth and technology. As marketing becomes synonymous with sales performance, the strategic dimension of a brand is left adrift.

Meanwhile, companies have become so focused on the technical—on data pipelines, platform migration, automation, and efficiency—systematically deprioritizing the intangibles that drive connection, trust, and value creation. Within companies, there's often no shared definition of what a brand strategy is, where strategic responsibility resides, or what outcomes it's designed to drive.

If Brand is to function as an interface between business and people, it first needs to be properly embedded in the company's operating system.

The Model of Growth Itself is Breaking
It's not just outdated strategy frameworks—the underlying model of growth they serve is breaking down. For decades Brand has operated in the service of volume-based, consumption-driven growth—referred to as Type 1 growth. Success was measured in market share, reach, impressions, and scale.

Consumer tension: The industrial era context that made Type 1 growth possible is shape-shifting. In countries like the United States, GDP growth is disproportionately driven by consumer spending, often accounting for 65-70% of total economic output. This GDP focus creates systemic pressure for companies to continue fuelling consumption, even as people face worsening inequality, cost of living, job security, ecological limits, and diminishing returns on material accumulation. The system that rewarded volume now undermines the well-being of the people it's meant to serve.

This structural tension is evident in consumer research. Interbrand's *Customer Arenas* work reveals that category boundaries are dissolving as people navigate life by intent, rather than product vertical. Gallup's Blind Spot report shows that many people feel unseen and emotionally disconnected, signalling a broader systemic failure in how institutions, including brands, interact with the people they serve.

Fatigue: We face mounting ecological constraints, cultural fatigue, economic inequality, and identity-driven backlash against over consumption. Consumer signals bear this out. According to Havas' Meaningful Brands study, 81% of people say they wouldn't care if most brands disappeared tomorrow. C Space's Thrive Paradox research adds dimension: only 43–52% of consumers believe brands can help them live a better life.

This growing gap between Brand intention and lived experience is eroding trust. People are not just tired of being marketed to—they're tired of being asked to care about brands that don't care about them. The emotional economy has moved from persuasion to proof. Consumers no longer reward virtue signalling or polished performance—they reward brands that create tangible value, enable participation, and seamlessly integrate into their lives.

Type 2 growth: Emerging is an economic transition from Type 1 to Type 2 growth: from extractive to generative. Type 2 growth focuses on creating value through depth, rather than scale. It rewards brands that build capacity, not just revenue. This might mean promoting better health outcomes, community participation, creativity, access, or even emotional resilience.

Brands stuck in Type 1 logic will find themselves pushing harder for smaller returns. Growth depends on brands recognizing that scale isn't enough—and while this may sound idealistic, continuing to rely on volume-based approaches is what's actually failing. Brand must become infrastructure: how companies operate, what they enable, and which systems they belong to.

As accessibility overtakes accumulation as a marker of prosperity, brands must redefine what it means to create value in people's lives. People aren't looking for more—they're looking for better: better systems, better participation, and better outcomes. When value isn't defined by ownership—Brand can no longer rely on positioning, image, belief, or purpose. It must function as a system designed to help people thrive.

For What Comes Next
This is not a call for better execution. It's a call for strategic reinvention. What brand strategy needs now is not refinement but redefinition: a new mental model, a new strategic imperative, new foundations.

The failures of Brand today are not failures of creativity or communication. They are structural. A discipline built for another era cannot keep pace with the complexity it must now handle.

The question is no longer whether brand strategy needs to change, but how we design that change for what comes next.

The path forward isn't about better execution of old models or minor refinements to inherited frameworks. It requires recognizing that we're entering an era defined not by what brands believe or the stories they tell, but by what they make possible—and how they inhabit that possibility.

permission TO REGRESS

When pressure mounted, we chose what was easy. Not what was right. Not what was possible. Just what was familiar.

The "Musk effect" normalized executive chaos. One high-profile rollback on climate commitments gave others cover. Privacy protections quietly eroded. Pandemic era health safeguards dissolved. Each reversal set a precedent: if they can pull back, so can we.

What looked like independent decisions felt like a coordinated and binary retreat from complexity.

The appeal was obvious: immediate cost savings with delayed consequences. Rolling back remote work was cheaper than building new collaborative systems and rethinking space. Cutting diversity programs eliminated "messy" conversations.

Easy money. Hard futures.
But regression isn't just corporate—it's cultural.

Democracy is under threat worldwide. Women's rights are eroding. Climate denial is resurgent. The pattern is consistent: when complexity rises, we retreat into false simplicity instead of building adaptive capacity.

We retrench in systems that no longer serve us because it feels safer than evolution. Old sytems. All failing. All familiar.

This tension can't hold. Either, we break toward possibility—investing in systems that enable human flourishing. Or we break toward regression—accepting that extraction and control are all we're capable of.

Regression has momentum. It's seductive. Profitable. But terminal.

Companies can't wait for better times or follow old playbooks. Those that build adaptive capacity—not those that squeeze efficiency from broken models will win.

Enabling Possibility

2

inheritance to inhabitance

We've arrived at the threshold.

So far, we've unpacked the layered history of brand strategy—the frameworks inherited, the limits of purpose, and the structural shifts now straining brand models. We've seen how meaning and function drifted apart, how brands were expected to matter more but given a short runway to do so. And we've recognised this isn't just a brand problem—it reflects fundamental changes in how people relate to institutions, value, and meaning.

Section two marks the beginning of addressing these changes—from brand as a static layer to brand as an adaptive system designed for the world ahead. Brand strategy must be designed forward—not only informed by what brands have been, but by what the world is becoming.

We explore the era of possibility—and the deeper forces influencing it. We'll look at:

- How this new era changes how meaning and value are created.

- How macro-drivers across spiritual, social, economic, technological, and emotional dimensions are reshaping commerce and culture.

- Why identifying key certainties and uncertainties matter—not to predict the future, but to expand strategic capacity.

- How foresight helps us surface blind spots, challenge assumptions, and understand brand's role in dynamic systems.

This isn't a futures textbook. It's a reorientation. We've already looked back to see what must be true for the present to take shape. Now we begin scanning forward—mapping the contours of what lies ahead and identifying how Brand must be designed to support what comes next.

Because the strategic structures we choose to inhabit will determine our capacity to navigate complexity and create value through what emerges.

the better WAY

In March 2020, when the world came to a standstill, we glimpsed something else.

Empty highways revealed cleaner air. Families rediscovered dinner tables. Communities organized mutual aid networks. Cities imagined streets without cars.

We began to ask: What if we didn't go back to normal? What if normal wasn't working?

For a brief moment, possibility felt tangible—not abstract or aspirational, but immediate and real. We could see a better way because we were living it, even if born from crisis.

But then recovery began. And recovery meant reverting.

The Leo Burnett Humankind study revealed what happened next: companies focused on getting "back to normal" instead of building toward what people had imagined. Companies that promised trans- formation delivered optimisation. Systems that showed flexibility snapped back to familiar patterns.

People could envision better outcomes, but couldn't participate in them. The enabling conditions weren't in place and the courage not sustainable.

Instead, we chose what was easy, familiar—and let's be honest—what was most profitable, all under the guise of healing.

This is the Thrive Paradox: We can imagine better outcomes, but we struggle to create the conditions that make them possible. We confuse inspiration with infrastructure.

But here's what we learned: possibility without enablement is just sentiment. And sentiment alone will never build the world we glimpsed when everything felt different.

The question isn't whether we can see a better way. We can. The question is whether we'll build it.

era of possibility

We are living in a moment defined by possibility—but also by contradiction.

The future feels infinite and fragile at once. One foot in science fiction, the other in systemic fragility. Extraordinary progress meets extraordinary pressure. Life is getting better and harder at the same time.

Breakthroughs abound: AI, quantum computing, mRNA therapies, fusion energy, space infrastructure. But alongside them: climate anxiety, media distrust, economic precarity, geopolitical volatility, and institutional decay.

People feel that dissonance. The pace of advancement is outstripping our ability to process it. This isn't an era that can be navigated through certainty.

It requires imagination. It demands possibility.

The Imagination Gap

While our cognitive IQ continues to rise, our collective imagination is flatlining, right when we need it most.

We've optimized systems for efficiency, not elasticity. Education rewards analytical reasoning over generative thought. Media cycles chase reaction, not reflection. Businesses prioritize productivity over new possibilities.

But imagination isn't a luxury—it's possibility by another name. It's the cognitive flexibility needed to navigate uncertainty and see beyond current market conditions and existing category dynamics.

While analytical intelligence solves known problems with known variables, imagination surfaces the problems we haven't named and the
solutions we haven't yet considered.

Expanding our Understanding

We are living with profound limitations in how we see the world, limits
that shape everything we think is possible.

Sociologist Fred Polak argued that a culture's vitality depends on the
health of its images of the future. When a society can envision flourishing
possibilities, culture blooms. When those images decay, so does culture
itself.

And yet, new knowledge arrives daily.

Archaeological discoveries reshape our sense of human history.
Extinct species reappear.
Plant intelligence reveals communication networks.

Our knowledge expands, but our cultural imagination often defaults to
dystopia or recycled sci-fi tropes. That gap constrains strategic thinking.

The era of possibility isn't about optimizing old answers—it's about asking new questions. When we accept the limits of what we know, we create
room for what we might learn. When we question the future we assume
is inevitable, we create space to design for more potential.

The Trust Trajectory

The first era of modern commerce was built on trust: dependability,
consistency, and stability. Brands signalled quality, while institutions
signalled reliability.

But eventually, trust became commoditized. When everyone promised
performance, differentiation shifted to meaning. Brand became belief.
Identity. Purpose.

Now, all three—trust, meaning, and function—are breaking down.

Brands make belief claims that they can't deliver. Institutions promise
progress they can't operationalize. Systems optimize performance while
degrading lived experience.

Possibility gives us the strategic space to rebuild both trust and meaning through action rather than promises. When brands enable possibility, trust emerges from what people can actually accomplish, not what companies claim to believe. Meaning gets reconstructed through tangible outcomes rather than aspirational statements.

Beyond Confidence: Why Possibility is Different
Traditional economics treats confidence as a leading indicator. Consumer confidence. Business optimism. Investor sentiment. These metrics extrapolate future behaviour from current conditions.

But possibility operates differently:

- Confidence is retrospective—it extrapolates from past performance

- Possibility is speculative—it creates space for outcomes that don't yet exist

- Confidence relies on predictable systems

- Possibility thrives in uncertainty

We're in a moment where confidence metrics are failing to explain behaviour. What's driving action now isn't confidence in the system—it's possibility-thinking *beyond* the system.

Consumption in Contradiction: New Cultural Behaviours
The breakdown between confidence and consumption isn't just economic—it's emotional. A new lexicon has emerged to capture the contradictions:

- "Vibecession" – Economic anxiety without a technical recession.

- "Doom spending" – Anxiety-fuelled consumption—escapist, not optimistic.

- "Cautious spender" – Strategic, values-driven, and deeply price-sensitive.

These aren't just internet terms. They're signals of a deeper shift: consumption is now driven less by confidence and more by a complex mix of emotion, survival, and deliberate self-determination. Even, "conscious consumption" isn't just about values—it's evolved into a coping mechanism. A way of exerting agency inside volatile and paradoxical systems.

In May 2024, U.S. consumer confidence jumped 12+ points—yet discretionary spending intentions dropped. The old correlation is breaking. And these paradoxes aren't isolated or limited to sentiment—they're rewiring the very mechanics of value creation.

One in particular is reshaping the strategic landscape more than any other: the collapse of the old scarcity–abundance cycle.

The Scarcity–Abundance Paradox

Scarcity and abundance have always co-existed. But until now, they cycled over time or split by place: feast and famine, expansion and contraction. You could plan for one without having to operate in the other at the same time.

Simultaneity: What's different now is that scarcity and abundance operate simultaneously within the same systems. A person might face housing scarcity while experiencing information abundance. A company might have abundant data but scarce talent. This simultaneity breaks traditional strategic logic and forces a non-binary approach to understanding value creation.

Historically, competition set the tone.

- In scarcity, the logic was to claim territory, defend resources, and maximise extraction.

- In abundance, it was to scale quickly, democratise access, and lower friction.

Optionality: You could choose a playbook, a fixed position, and stick to it. When both states operate at once, the old playbooks work against each other—optimizing for one immediately undermines the other. Brand strategy can no longer optimize for single conditions. It must help organizations and people navigate between contradictory states - making optionality and navigation strategic capabilities.

Three current expressions of the paradox:

1. **Physical scarcity + digital abundance**
Climate change and fragile supply chains constrain materials like coffee, chocolate, lithium, and clean water—while digital tools, media, and platforms replicate infinitely.
Brand implication: In scarce domains, protect and expand access; in abundant ones, curate, filter, and add meaning.

2. **Attention scarcity + content abundance**
More content is created every minute than anyone could consume in a lifetime—yet coherent, meaningful attention is rare and costly.
Brand implication: Stop adding to the noise; design systems that filter, signal quality, and earn focus.

3. **Capability abundance + context scarcity**
AI puts powerful tools in everyone's hands, but contextual intelligence—knowing when, where, and why to act is scarce.
Brand implication: Build context into your offering; guide timing, intent, and application.

In this environment, you can't optimize for scarcity without affecting abundance—or vice versa. The advantage now lies in enabling people to move between the two with fluency.

Why This Shapes the Era of Possibility
The Era of Possibility isn't defined by optimism—it's defined by conditions that expand and constrain at the same time. The scarcity-abundance paradox is one of its most profound features: a structural rewiring that makes navigation, not control, a source of strategic advantage.

Brands that master this don't just survive the paradox—they expand what's possible within it, giving people the clarity, agency, and optionality to operate across shifting conditions. That is what turns paradox into possibility.

This collapse of the old scarcity–abundance cycle is one example of how the Era of Possibility defies linear logic. To work inside these conditions, we need more fluency in how we think about value creation and the future itself.

That fluency—the ability to navigate contradictory conditions—is exactly why the scarcity–abundance paradox belongs at the heart of the Era of Possibility.

The Spectrum of Stretch
To navigate an era defined by contradictions, we need better tools for thinking about the future. Most strategic planning operates within narrow bands of likelihood—extrapolating from current and past trends or benchmarking against competitors. But when systems are breaking down and reforming simultaneously, this approach misses where real opportunity lives.

Possibility operates across a spectrum that expands how we frame strategic options:

- **Probable:** What's most likely based on current trajectories. This is where most brands operate—incremental improvements, predictable market moves, safe bets that feel strategic but rarely create breakthrough advantage.

- **Plausible**: What could unfold with moderate shifts in conditions. Here's where smart brands start to differentiate—anticipating regulatory changes, demographic shifts, or technology adoption curves before competitors catch on.

- **Possible:** What becomes achievable when we stretch current systems or thinking. This requires imagination and innovation. It's where Tesla positioned electric vehicles before infrastructure existed, or where Patagonia built a business model around planned obsolescence's opposite.

- **Preferable:** The futures we actively want to create, regardless of current likelihood. This isn't wishful thinking—it's intentional direction-setting that can actually shift what becomes probable over time.

But consider this: who gets to define what's "realistic" at each level decides what gets imagined in the first place. What seems impossible to established players may be obvious to newcomers. What feels plausible in Silicon Valley may seem absurd in rural communities, and vice versa.

For brands, this means two things. First, your strategic advantage increasingly lies in the "possible" zone—imagining solutions that stretch current systems without breaking them entirely. Second, expanding who's involved in that imagining process isn't just about inclusion—it's about accessing possibilities that homogeneous or biased thinking literally cannot see (or don't want to see).

The scarcity-abundance paradox we're experiencing is one example of why this expanded thinking matters. Traditional planning tools assume you're operating in one condition or the other. But when both operate simultaneously, breakthrough strategy requires imagining across the full spectrum—from probable scarcity responses to preferable abundance outcomes, often at the same time.

Possibility is the most expansive and generative zone—it's where the other three can actually emerge and develop. The "probable" zone has become narrow and unreliable when contradictions operate simultaneously. The "preferable" zone, while important for direction-setting, can feel disconnected from practical action when systems are volatile. And "plausible" often just splits the difference without expanding what's actually achievable.

But the "possible" zone creates the expansive space where all futures perspectives can live and develop. It's open enough to generate new probabilities, flexible enough to accommodate multiple preferences, and imaginative enough to stretch what seems plausible. It's not just another strategic option—it's the generative condition that makes the others more robust and actionable.

The era demands this expansive starting point because when everything else feels constrained or contradictory, possibility creates the cognitive and strategic room to work with what's emerging rather than just managing what's breaking down.

Understanding this spectrum is one thing. Operating within it strategically is another.

New Strategic Capabilities
We're no longer in an era where *purpose* is enough.

The strategic questions aren't "How do we stand out?" or "Why do we exist?" They're aligned to, "How do we enable possibility for people?"

Brands face a choice: Optimise broken systems or Enable new ones.

The first delivers diminishing returns.
The second enables transformation.

This requires movement towards *adaptive capacity.* Adaptive capacity is the ability to sense change, adjust quickly, and ma ntain coherence while evolving. Unlike optimisation—which makes existing systems run better—adaptive capacity builds the capability to thrive in conditions you can't predict or control. It's what allows brands to remain relevant as contexts shift, rather than becoming obsolete when their original assumptions break down. Adaptive capacity relies on meaning and function working together and requires Brand to become infrastructure.

This infrastructure approach signals a critical inflection point. When brands function as adaptive systems rather than static messages, it's not enough to sell optimism or project values. Value must be constructed differently—across systemic, social, and individual dimensions—creating outcomes people can experience, not just beliefs they can adopt.

Possibility is Practical
Possibility might sound abstract—but it's the most practical response to systemic breakdown.

When frameworks fail, possibility creates the space—cognitively, emotionally, structurally—to design new ones.

It's not wishful thinking. It's sense-making. It's strategic and anticipatory thinking about what doesn't yet exist.

But alone, it's not enough. It needs a strategic response—one that can be translated into action, systems, and structures that work with what's emerging rather than what's breaking down.

enablement

The Era of Possibility isn't just a description of what's happening around us—it's the new frontier to navigate. When contradictions operate simultaneously, when people navigate both scarcity and abundance, when systems require both stability and elast city, possibility becomes the only orientation that can hold these tensions productively. And enablement is the only strategic response that works within this environment—for both the people brands serve and for the brands themselves.

While purpose-driven strategy tries to resolve contradictions by taking positions, enablement thrives within them by expanding what becomes possible. This isn't just better strategy; it's how brands create sustainable growth.

Purpose tried to make brands matter more.
Enablement makes them useful again.

How We Exist

This reorientation shifts brand strategy from *why we exist* to *how we exist*—from belief carrier to capacity creator. Enablement is how brands create value by expanding what becomes possible for people and organisations. It's not about "helping." It's about structuring value through the deliberate design of conditions that expand what people and businesses can do, be, achieve, and solve.

The Shift from Social to Generative Economics (*Fig. 2*)	
Purpose	**Enablement**
"Why do we exist"	"How do we exist"
Social economics	Generative economics
Values alignment	Value expansion
Intent-based conviction	Meaning-based outcomes

From Social to Generative

Moving from social to generative economics marks a fundamental move away from the Purpose Era—monetising alignment with beliefs, social behaviours, movements, and causes. Success meant converting social signals into brand affinity.

Generative economics works differently. It doesn't monetise existing values—it creates new capacity. Instead of extracting value from cultural alignment, brands create value by expanding what people can do, be, or solve.

Enablement resolves the core tension between meaning and function. When brands focus on how they exist—as systems, as operations, as daily realities—meaning and function become interconnected rather than competing priorities.

From Optimisation to Enablement

This requires a fundamentally different approach to strategy. Many organisations are still optimising inside broken systems. But optimisation assumes the system is sound. When the system itself is flawed, it becomes counterproductive.

Enablement operates from a different logic. Instead of making broken systems run better, it creates the conditions for new systems and outcomes to emerge—building functional integrity through structural innovation rather than incremental fixes.

Consider the difference:

Optimisation: "How do we make our loyalty program more engaging?"
Enablement: "How do we create the conditions for customers to build skills, connections, or capabilities they value?"

The first extracts more value from existing behaviour. The second expands what becomes possible and builds adaptive capacity.

Two-Way Value Creation

Traditional models extract value from users—they consume what brands produce. Enablement creates two-way value, where users contribute meaningfully while receiving tangible benefit in return.

Examples:

- Duolingo: Users gain language skills; Duolingo learns from user patterns to improve the system for all.

- Nike Run Club: Runners get coaching and community; Nike gains insight to shape future products and support.

- Raspberry Pi: Users access affordable computing; the brand enables an ecosystem of makers and educators.

- Le Page Building Supplies: Retired contractors mentor younger teams passing on decades of knowledge; the company gains quality outcomes and community resilience.

Enablement makes people participants, not just beneficiaries. Both matter, but participation builds systems that scale and stretch. It asks brands to focus on better outcomes—not just for customers, but for culture, commerce, and community.

The New Strategic Imperative

Enabling possibility is not a philosophical ideal. It's a new strategic imperative. It answers the question: "What comes after purpose?" And it answers it with a more systemic and generative one: "How can we enable possibility for people?"

This single question connects brand strategy to business, brings a futures lens, and demands a systems approach.

Enablement is a response to macro forces influencing commerce, culture, and human consumption. From technological acceleration to spiritual inquiry to economic fragmentation, the signals are clear: legacy brand models aren't sufficient for what's emerging.

In the next chapter, we explore the macro-drivers making enablement not just preferable—but necessary. And what they reveal about the world brands must now learn to inhabit.

participation ECONOMY

The marketing industry misunderstood the participation economy—systems where people co-create value, not just consume it. It equated participation with brand engagement—likes, shares, clicks, follows. Participation became a tactic, a KPI.

Brands asked how people could interact with them, not what they were enabling people to do.

But participation isn't just interaction. True participation is agentic: you don't just feed the system—you shape it. And today, many people don't want visible participation at all.

The spectrum now includes: the opt-in consumer, the selective engager, the passive observer, the untrackable user, and the platform refugee. All are valid. All must be designed for.

This is why enablement must sit above participation. If systems are designed to deliver value, access, and agency, participation will follow. But it might not. And that's okay.

Consider the difference: LEGO Ideas lets people decide what gets made. Shopify enables sellers, not just sales. Patagonia customers advocate for environmental policy. These aren't just engaged audiences—they're collaborators in systems.

When participation is structured well, it creates economic feedback loops: people contribute value and receive value in return—through data, revenue, capabilities, access, or recognition. This isn't engagement; it's value exchange.

Brands win when they enable new forms of possibility—not those who get louder applause, but those who give people the tools and protocols to act meaningfully. If we want people to opt-in, we need to give them something worth opting into.

When brands do that, they don't just invite participation—they enable different outcomes.

what's shaping futures?

We live in a time of accelerated possibility and compounding pressure. The macro-drivers shaping our world today—technological evolution, ecological disruption, changing value systems, and behavioural contradiction—represent structural shifts, asking brands to think bigger, act bolder, and design differently.

Before we examine the eight forces reshaping the future, we need to ground ourselves in the human systems already under strain—and in the emergent logic rising in response.

Meaning now has to be lived, not just stated. The breakdown of institutional trust hasn't left a void—it's activated a new kind of meaning-making, built through rituals, tools, and systems that help people live with intention.

Brands that once relied on belief must now be built for practice.

As cultural coherence fractures, people reach for micro-systems that offer rhythm, perspective, and identity—often mediated through commerce. This isn't a new wave of purpose. It's a shift toward embedded value systems—systems people can use, not just believe in.

Identity is no longer fixed or declared—it's navigated. People don't see themselves through stable roles, but through dynamic participation across communities, platforms, and economies.

Consumption is now entangled with belonging and agency is shared, negotiated—and sometimes automated.

This produces both fragmentation of culture and reassembly of influence. Strategies that treat people as static segments or owned audiences will miss the fluid power dynamics shaping tomorrow's markets.

We're also living through an emotional infrastructure crisis.

Burnout isn't just personal—it's systemic.
People don't want more content, more choice, more interaction.
They want pacing, regulation, recovery.

In this context, emotional design becomes a strategic asset. Brands are being judged not just by tone, but by tempo. Mood is no longer a tactic—it's a threshold for attention and participation.

Meanwhile, our most advanced technologies are colliding with our most outdated systems. AI agents and predictive platforms promise seamless futures, even as basic needs remain unmet.

It's the paradox of innovation without integration. Growth logic clashes with economic precarity. And people are beginning to choose differently—shifting from ownership to access, from extraction to care.

The next strategic frontier is about designing for the systemic conditions of life.

That's why we begin here—with the forces that shape possibility. Because if these shifts are reshaping how people live, work, spend, connect, and define value, then brand strategy must evolve accordingly.

Eight Forces Shaping Possibility
These aren't trends. They're the evolving structures of life, shaping not just what people want, but what systems they need. And they're what brand strategy must now address.

Infrastructure Collapse

Systems exhaustion: The infrastructure that once supported communication, commerce, and cultural coherence are breaking down. Media channels are fragmented. Institutions are distrusted. Interfaces are overloaded. Brands are no longer guaranteed access, reach, or relevance—not because people have tuned out, but because the infrastructure they relied on has fractured.

Advertising effectiveness has sharply declined. Traditional channels are saturated or bypassed entirely. Trust in institutional messaging—from governments to global brands—has eroded in the wake of performative virtue, misinformation, and overexposure. People aren't tuning out from apathy—they're tuning out from exhaustion. In this environment, attention is no longer something brands can buy—it's something they must earn, contextually and relationally.

> The 2023 Edelman Trust Barometer found that only 42% of people globally trust advertising—and 76% actively avoid it online when given the option.

Digital infrastructure shifts: Digital infrastructure is being rewired in real time. Cookies are crumbling. Algorithms are mutating. Platforms are splintering into smaller, less visible spaces. Dark social—encrypted chats, private groups, shared docs, untrackable threads—has become the real engine of digital culture. The distributed web is inching closer to the mainstream, with signals like blockchain wallets, token-based access, and the early adoption of Web3 protocols shaping what participation and identity may look like in the next cycle. Even retail is being reshaped: retail media networks are quietly becoming power brokers in commerce infrastructure, merging marketing, transaction, and behavioural data into privatized ad ecosystems that brands must now navigate.

But this isn't just a comms problem. It's a breakdown of the shared scaffolding that once connected people to brands, media to culture, companies to communities. As infrastructure collapses, people are building direct pathways: from creators to consumers, from brand to micro-community, from person to product. This shift has enabled new models—such as DTC, decentralized platforms, and social-led businesses—but it has also revealed a deeper need: for brands to create systems that people want to opt into, rather than relying on visibility alone. Opt-in has limits—people can't engage deeply with every brand, nor do they want to. Relevance now requires not just access, but discernment and restraint.

Interface evolution: Interfaces are evolving as well. Tangible technologies—sensors, ambient devices, adaptive surfaces—are blending the physical and digital in ways that feel less like tech and more like texture. Mixed-reality environments are emerging, from spatial computing to augmented layers in everyday objects. In the wake of surveillance marketing, people are demanding not just transparency, but also consent, and control. The backlash to algorithmic manipulation is creating space for something quieter: interactions grounded in usefulness, permission, and presence.

For strategy, the implications are clear: when infrastructure breaks down, interaction must be rebuilt from the inside out. Brand meaning must now be embedded in use—not just assumed in message. The ecosystem must carry the value, not just the campaign. And brands must operate not as broadcasters, but as participatory systems that offer coherence, connection, and optionality inside a fragmented world.

Fluid Living Systems

Dissolving boundaries: The structures that once defined how, where, and when we live are breaking down. Work, home, identity, age, and even time are becoming more malleable—less linear, less locatable, less predictable. What's emerging in their place is a logic of fluidity: a life architecture that flexes to context, preference, and circumstance rather than conforming to industrial-era norms. Life no longer follows a single script. It moves more like overlapping layers in motion than separate categories.

No fixed states: People no longer live in fixed geographies or static routines. They navigate between cities, time zones, devices, and social environments—often simultaneously. Work and home have merged, giving rise to hybrid lifestyles, modular spaces, and mobile micro-environments. The home is now a modular interface: workspace, wellness hub, entertainment portal, service centre, sanctuary. Living systems now extend beyond individuals to include ambient technologies, connected platforms, and shared consumption models that toggle between personal and collective use.

 The rise of portfolio careers, project-based economies, and creator-driven income streams is further decentering the 9-to-5 model. Location independence is no longer the domain of digital nomads—it's increasingly a mainstream aspiration.

But fluidity extends beyond logistics. The boundaries of life phases themselves are shifting. People are parenting later, retiring earlier—or not at all. Identity is no longer tethered to traditional milestones. Agelessness, multi-potentiality, and neurodiversity are reframing what "normal" looks like. People are curating their own rhythms, rejecting outdated success templates, and treating flexibility as foundational.

Meanwhile, systems are struggling to keep up. Most public infrastructure, corporate benefits, and commercial experiences are still designed around a fixed user model. But people now expect services that follow them, not the other way around. From on-demand care to subscription-based access, the most effective systems are those that meet people where they are—and shift with them. That means fluid systems aren't just consumer preferences—they're structural imperatives.

> A 2023 Deloitte report found 63% of global workers would consider leaving a job that didn't support flexibility in schedule and location.

Context switching: The same expectations apply to brands. People want seamless transitions between contexts—digital to physical, work to leisure, solo to shared. They want products and services that adapt to life's shifting contours. In this landscape, consistency doesn't mean sameness—it means coherence across changing conditions.

For brands, the challenge is to operate like a living system—one that moves with people, flexes to their context, and maintains integrity while evolving its form. This means designing experiences that are modular, interoperable, and attuned to the soft signals of life as it's lived. Brands that still rely on rigid journeys or fixed user personas will increasingly feel misaligned with their customers. The future belongs to brands that understand: fluidity isn't a trend—it's the baseline condition for relevance.

Self-Sovereignty

Reclaiming control: For decades, people traded their data, decisions, and digital identities to platforms, institutions, and intermediaries in exchange for convenience or access. But the pendulum is swinging. Across technology, commerce, and lifestyle, a new ethos is taking hold—one that prioritizes personal agency, privacy, direct access, and the right to define and manage one's own systems. Self-sovereignty is evolving from ideology to design principle.

Self-sovereignty isn't merely about resisting surveillance capitalism—it's about fundamentally rebalancing power. People want more than transparency, they want tools that allow them to opt in, not be tracked by default. The expectation is shifting from passive terms-of-service acceptance to active control over data, identity, access, and participation. From ad blockers to password managers to decentralized IDs, the toolkit of digital self-governance is expanding rapidly. Even mainstream platforms are now responding, adding granular privacy controls and permission layers. Not from altruism, but from demand.

Restructured identity: More than just data, identity itself is being restructured. The old model—one person, one profile, one platform—no longer applies. People now manage multiple identities across networks, platforms, and contexts. In some cases, they want anonymity; in others, hyper-personalization. Identity is being treated as a resource—something to be protected, remixed, or monetized. This restructuring has implications that extend beyond technology, affecting healthcare, finance, education, and citizenship. Systems that assume static identities are breaking down in the face of people who expect flexble, context-aware, self-determined control.

A 2023 McKinsey Digital Trust report found that 71% of consumers are more likely to buy from companies that give them control over how their data is used, yet only 21% believe brands are delivering it.

Intentional interaction design: This movement is also reshaping how people engage with brands. There's a growing intolerance for manipulative design, coercive personalization, and one-way communication. People want direct access to content, services, communities, and commerce, without platform friction or marketing noise. They're gravitating toward experiences where participation is consensual and value flows both ways. And they're using increasingly sophisticated tools to curate their inputs, choosing when, where, and how brands can enter their lives.

What's emerging is a logic of intentional interaction. Whether it's the rise of indie tech stacks, community-owned platforms, or customizable personal AI agents, the future is pointing toward people owning the structure of their digital lives. But it's not just about controlling access—it's about creating autonomously. DIY technology and self-directed production are transforming the way people interact with brands. Consumers are no longer asking, "What do you make?" They're asking, "What do you make possible for me to make?"

User agency: From open-source filters and creative blueprints to customizable APIs and make-it-yourself formulations, people are turning to brands for modular frameworks they can remix. Templates, prompts, toolkits, and logic systems are replacing products as the value layer. The rise of creative AI has only accelerated this: with the right structure, anyone can now generate an image, remix a flavour, build a playlist, or code a utility. The Star Trek replicator metaphor isn't far off—it's not about choosing from what's offered, but generating what's needed, in context.

A 2024 survey by CivicScience found that 46% of Gen Z and Millennials say they would prefer to "co-create or customize" a product with a brand than simply buy it off the shelf.

For brands, this requires a deep strategic shift: from building for audience reach to building for user agency. Systems must now be designed with clear opt-in pathways, interoperable identity frameworks, permissions and modular tools for contribution and customization. Self-sovereignty isn't a fringe demand—it's the new baseline for participation. In this landscape, the most future-ready brands won't deliver fixed solutions. They'll enable generative ones.

Participatory Economics

New architecture: The architecture of value creation is being rewritten—from top-down production to bottom-up participation. People are no longer just consumers—they are co-creators, curators, investors, and community stewards. The economy is becoming participatory—not just in principle, but in infrastructure. New tools, platforms, and incentives let individuals and communities build and share value directly, without institutional permission.

Fandoms have become economic engines. From K-pop stars coordinating global charitable campaigns to Roblox creators earning real incomes from digital skins, people are organizing themselves into creative micro-markets. The line between audience and builder is dissolving. Whether through content remixing, world-building, or social trading, participation is now a form of production, not just interaction.

Shared value: At the same time, new systems of shared value are emerging. Mutual aid, co-ops, DAO-like governance models, and community-owned IP are no longer niche experiments—they're expanding as people seek alternatives to extractive platforms and asymmetrical reward systems. Participation isn't always visible or performative. Sometimes it's silent, embedded, or relational— strengthening a system's resilience rather than fuelling a moment's virality. But the logic is consistent: those who contribute should benefit.

Lived complexity: Traditional business models are under pressure. As digital decentralization rises and trust in corporations declines, people are increasingly drawn to systems that offer them agency, voice, and upside. Value is no longer "delivered"—it's shaped in motion. Participatory ecosystems—whether based on shared ownership, creative input, or micro-contributions—are setting new expectations for how value is built and shared. While Gen Z and Millennials are often credited with this shift, it's Gen X that has long operated at the fault line—first to navigate collapsing legacy systems, last to receive institutional support. Now in midlife, many Gen Xers are quietly reshaping cultural and economic models to fit new definitions of worth, work, and belonging—from done-by-midnight dance parties to alternative third spaces, remix communities, and slow-grown creative careers. This isn't just generational adaptation—it's structural evolution driven by lived complexity.

> According to Influencer Marketing Hub (2024), over 200 million people globally now identify as part of the "creator economy" with many earning income or access through participation rather than formal employment.

For brands, this requires a strategic shift: from audience engagement to ecosystem orchestration. It's not about asking people to "interact"—it's about building the conditions in which participation creates mutual value. Brands that treat communities as a distribution channel will lose relevance. The future belongs to brands that create roles, frameworks, and co-creation mechanisms that allow people to contribute meaningfully, be recognized equitably, and shape the system alongside the brand.

Identity Capital

Fluid identity: Identity has become fluid, assembled, and strategic. It is no longer a fixed state defined by demographics or life stage, but rather a collection of active signals, affiliations, and contexts that shift across platforms, spaces, and moods. In this new landscape, people don't just have identities—they construct them, remix them, and leverage them as forms of social and economic capital. Identity is not only who you are—it's how you move through the world, what you signal, what you select, and who you're seen with.

Shared codes: These are reshaping consumption in profound ways. People increasingly shop through the lens of identity, seeking products and experiences that affirm or project who they are (or who they want to be). Purchases are made for signalling, for alignment, for experimentation—not just to serve a function. Communities of belonging are formed less through ownership and more through shared codes, cultural references, values, or inside language. Belonging itself has become ambient and distributed, performed as much through interaction, creation, and commentary as through acquisition.

The act of consumption is no longer the end of the journey—it's part of a continuous feedback loop. Whether it's co-designing a product, remixing a brand's message, or translating an aesthetic across spaces, people are actively editing and extending the brands they connect with. Prompts, toolkits, templates, and style architectures are becoming embedded into brand ecosystems, giving users a way to build with and through the brand. In this context, identity becomes not just expressive, but constructive.

Identity terrains: Meanwhile, expectations are evolving. People no longer want to be assigned personas or funnelled into archetypes—they expect brands to flex with their context. What someone shares on LinkedIn may not align with their TikTok persona, gaming avatar, or private Discord life. Identity is contextual and emotionally layered. Gender, age, ability, aesthetic, belief—these are no longer "targets," they're terrains. Brands that attempt to categorize people into fixed roles or assume coherence across different contexts will be ignored—or rejected.

> According to a 2023 GWI report, 52% of GenZ say their identity "changes depending on the environment they're in"—a 30% increase from five years prior.

A new brand role is emerging—not identity as narrative, but identity as infrastructure. Brands should stop trying to define who people are and instead become adaptive tools for people to define and express themselves. That means creating fluid interfaces, modular systems, and values that can be interpreted rather than dictated. In a world of ambient identity, the most relevant brands won't own the message—they'll offer the canvas to shape it.

Augmented Intelligence

Ambient tech: The integration of artificial intelligence into everyday life is no longer speculative—it's ambient. From AI assistants managing schedules to predictive platforms streamlining choices, intelligence is shifting from something we control to something that runs in the background and co-acts with us. These tools don't just automate—they anticipate. They absorb friction, triage decisions and manage complexity. And increasingly, they serve not just tasks, but identity.

What began as intelligent search and voice interfaces is evolving into agentic systems—tools that act on our behalf based on goals, preferences, and emotional cues. They help choose meals, organize routines, generate communications, and negotiate micro-decisions across health, commerce, and content. While enterprise use of AI dominates headlines, it's this quiet integration into daily life that's reshaping the human experience. And it's already changing the way people interact with brands.

Co-navigating choice: People are no longer navigating choices alone—they're co-navigating with machines. AI companions, personal recommendation systems, and context-aware interfaces are shaping not just what people see, but what they choose. Co-piloting creates a new kind of influence economy—one in which attention isn't just scarce, it's intermediated. Brands aren't just appealing to people, they're appealing to their proxies. And these proxies are increasingly tuned to optimize for well-being, relevance, trust, and simplicity—not novelty or hype.

Co-navigation will reframe how loyalty, memory, and presence are built. People may remember a brand, but if their assistant doesn't, it won't matter. It creates pressure for brands to be legible, interoperable, and functional within agentic systems. Structure, metadata, and machine-readable logic now shape visibility and accessibility. AI isn't replacing human intention—it's restructuring the scaffolding that surrounds it.

Human enhancement: At the same time, collaboration with AI is becoming aspirational. It's not just about convenience—it's about capability. People are using generative tools to ideate, produce, co-create, and enhance output. From personalized content to AI-styled fashion, augmentation is becoming cultural, not just technical. And critically, this shift is democratizing ability—levelling barriers to creation, communication, and access for those previously excluded. AI is enabling neurodivergent users to organize thoughts, non-designers to visualize ideas, and time-poor individuals to complete tasks with greater autonomy. It's not replacing people—it's expanding who gets to participate, and how.

> In 2024, a Pew Research study found that 41% of Millennials and Gen Z use AI daily, not just for productivity, but for decision support, creativity, and life management.

For brands, this creates a dual imperative: design for collaboration and design for cognition. Tools, systems, and products must now interface seamlessly with human-AI hybrids. Brands that treat intelligence as a performance feature will be outpaced by those who treat it as a co-agent of everyday life—and an enabler of broader human access, contribution, and expression.

(Re)Generative Impact

Beyond people: We've reached the edge of sustainability as a strategic endpoint. For decades, "doing less harm" has been the default goal—offsetting footprints, minimizing waste, and reducing environmental impact. But the cultural centre of gravity is moving. The next frontier isn't sustainability—it's regeneration: the capacity to contribute back, repair systems, and design models that restore rather than extract. In this emerging landscape, the question isn't "Is this responsible?" It's "Does this make things better—for more than just the buyer?"

This shift is both attitudinal and infrastructural in nature. People are no longer satisfied with symbolic commitments or low-grade greenwashing. They're looking for material evidence of circularity, accountability, and system-level contribution. Circular design is becoming increasingly normalized across various industries, including fashion, food, packaging, and product lifecycles. Brands are developing second-life programs, material recapture strategies, and resale or refurbishment loops—not just to reduce waste, but to design longevity into their economic models. The logic is shifting: products are no longer endpoints—they're inputs for the next cycle.

Emotional memory: At the same time, a new layer of aspiration is emerging—not around status or luxury, but around emotional sustainability. Story, memory, and meaning are being reinserted into the consumption process. People are gravitating toward objects with history or imagination—items that feel heirloom-worthy, curated, remixed, or consciously upcycled. Nostalgia, narrative, and aesthetic care are becoming signals of value. Ironically, even fast fashion giants like Zara and H&M are embracing this ethos, introducing curated collections, second-hand integrations, and story-led capsule drops to respond to this cultural undercurrent.

This doesn't mean everyone is living a minimalist, zero-waste life. The aspiration toward regenerative impact is layered with real-world complexity: affordability gaps, access challenges, lifestyle trade-offs. But the trajectory is clear. People are trying to make better choices, expecting brands to meet them halfway. Increasingly, environmental logic is being fused with social value: labour practices, local supply chains, and community reciprocity. In other words, climate is no longer separable from culture.

Considered choices: Post-growth thinking is gaining traction, particularly among younger generations, who recognize the limitations of infinite growth on a finite planet. This mindset is redefining value, shifting from mass production to considered production, from efficiency to resilience, and from ownership to stewardship. Performance now encompasses lifecycle impact, systemic contribution, and social context—not just product function.

> A 2024 GlobeScan report found that 73% of global consumers believe brands should take an active role in addressing environmental and social problems, not just through philanthropy, but also through their operational practices.

For brands, this creates a design imperative: build systems that give more than they take, across time, people, and planet. Regenerative models aren't just reputational shields; they're operational advantages. Brands that embed circular logic, transparency, and reciprocal value into their models will not only earn cultural relevance—they'll be structurally aligned with the future of commerce.

Conscious Living

Quality of life: The very structure of aspiration is shifting. The post-industrial script—success as accumulation, productivity as progress, value as speed—is being quietly dismantled. In its place, a broader, more integrated concept is emerging: quality of life as the ultimate metric. Across generations, people are reassessing what matters—not only in the abstract, but in daily decisions, relationships, time use, and consumption patterns. And brands that once promised more are being asked to deliver meaningful.

But this shift isn't entirely a choice—it's a response to strain. Rising costs of living, emotional fatigue, burnout, and the erosion of public services have prompted people to reassess what is worth their energy, time, and money. Scale no longer feels safe. Performance no longer feels rewarding. In many cases, more has become unliveable. People are seeking alternative ways to live, not as a rebellion, but as a means of recalibration and survival. The pursuit of quality is not just aspirational—it's compensatory. It emerges as a necessary counterbalance to systems that no longer serve human life well.

Recalibration of definitions: This recalibration shows up everywhere. Ownership is no longer the pinnacle of access. From cars to couches to content, rental, reuse, and shared models are becoming increasingly normal. Younger consumers, often priced out of traditional asset ownership, are designing flexible lives centred on experiences, portability, and adaptability. Simultaneously, we're seeing a backlash to hustle culture and burnout economics. Success is no longer about visible output, but internal well-being. Emotional regulation, life pacing, and the ability to say "no" are becoming the new markers of status.

This redefinition of value is not only psychological—it's structural. Health isn't just physical, it's emotional and environmental. Consumption isn't just choice—it's care. That's why conscious spending is rising—not always frugal, but always more reflective. People aren't abandoning luxury; they're reinterpreting it. Quality, longevity, ethical production, and regenerative systems now sit beside prestige and performance. The rise of mood-first environments, sensory design, and therapeutic aesthetics points to a broader reorientation: how it feels is as important as what it does.

Unbound aging: Layered within this is a cultural and generational shift around ageing and care. The concept of a "no-age society" is emerging, in which self-actualization, contribution, and aesthetic preferences are no longer age-bound. Living models are evolving—from co-living and collective care to multigenerational households and integrated housing. Longevity isn't just about living longer—it's about living better, with more dignity, access, and joy across life phases.

> A 2024 Euromonitor survey found that 71% of global respondents say they are actively reevaluating what matters most—and changing how they spend and live as a result. For Millennials and Gen Z, over half now consider "peace of mind" more important than financial success.

For brands, the implication is clear: products and services must now contribute directly to quality of life, not just performance metrics. Whether that means simplifying routines, improving accessibility, softening emotional tone, or enabling richer ways to live, the brief has changed. Brand value will be measured by how it protects time, restores energy, supports care, and aligns with people's evolving priorities. In this world, to be relevant is to be nourishing, whether that's through care models or absurdist humour.

What The Future Demands of Brand

These eight macro-drivers we've just reviewed aren't predictions. They're intersecting conditions—the evolving weather systems of culture, commerce, and identity in which brand strategy must now operate.

Together, they signal a deeper shift: the infrastructure of how people live, work, and make meaning is being reconfigured. Brand must evolve—not just to respond, but to enable what comes next.

The Collective Signal
Across all eight drivers, a consistent pattern emerges:

- People are reclaiming agency

- Systems are becoming more fluid

- Infrastructure is fragmenting

- Participation is expanding

- Control is shifting from institutions to individuals—even as interdependence deepens

These aren't contradictions. They're signals of complexity. And complexity demands that brands operate as systems, not static assets.

Five Strategic Demands

1. **Elasticity:** Traditional brand strategy is too rigid for what's next. The strongest strategies won't just scale—they'll stretch across immediate needs and long-term conditions.

2. **Value Generation:** The extractive growth logic of past decades is collapsing under social and ecological strain. The new imperative is to generate multi-dimensional value across systems.

3. **Trust-as-a-Service:** Trust is no longer built through repetition. It's earned through responsiveness. Brands must become dynamic trust systems—credible, contextual, and useful as conditions shift.

4. **Participation:** People are no longer passive audiences—they're curators, collaborators, and co-builders. Brands must move beyond engagement tactics to build real mechanisms of inclusion and agency.

5. **Systemic Design:** Brand can no longer function as a narrative layer alone. They must function with a systems design mindset—shaping how value is created, exchanged, and experienced through the ecosystem, not necessarily the brand itself.

The Strategic Challenge
These aren't future shifts. They're already reshaping how people live, buy, belong, and build. These drivers aren't constraints. They're invitations to think systemically, act structurally, and imagine better.

The question is no longer, "Will brand strategy need to change?"
It's "How quickly can it adapt to enable what the future requires?"

But these macro-drivers don't play out evenly. They manifest differently across contexts, markets, and moments in time. To understand what that means for brand strategy, we turn to exploring different future scenarios, each creating distinct operating conditions.

What follows are four strategic scenarios—brand worlds that explore how these forces might reshape the brand's role, logic, and relationship to people.

They are not forecasts.
They are provocations—to stress-test assumptions and stretch imagination.

Let's explore what happens when brands respond—and what happens when they don't.

Eight Macro-Drivers Shaping the Era of Possibility (*Fig. 3*)	
Macro-Driver	**Key Supporting Drivers**
Infrastructure Collapse	Trust erosion in media and institutions, platform and channel fragmentation, rise of tangible tech and mixed-reality interfaces
Fluid Living Systems	Location-independent living, portfolio careers and home-work blending, ageless society and life phase fluidity
Self-Sovereignty Emergence	Data ownership and consent layers, DIY tools and self-directed production, multi-identity navigation and prompt-based systems
Participatory Economics	Fandoms as economic engines, distributed value creation through communities, participation-based and co-owned revenue models
Identity Capital	Contextual and performative identity, consumption as self-signalling, brands as adaptive identity infrastructure
Augmented Intelligence	Agentic AI systems and decision support, human-AI collaboration in everyday life, machine-readable brand architecture
(Re)Generative Impact	Circular economy and product recapture, emotional sustainability and meaningful objects, environmental and social value integration
Conscious Living	Conscious spending and emotional economy, accessibility over ownership, collective care and mood-responsive living systems

the changing shape of brand relationships

Brand relationships are changing—but not in ways many companies are prepared for. This isn't just a shift from digital to more digital, or from broadcast to social. It's a deeper transition: from brands as symbol or story, to brand as system.

The same tensions reappear:
Meaning versus function.
Centralization versus decentralization.
Performance versus participation.

One thing is certain: brands will continue to operate across fragmented ecosystems spanning platforms, identities, channels, and interaction modes.

What's uncertain is how people will choose to engage, what role they'll allow brands to play, and whether brands can adapt in time.

Building the Scenarios
The four scenarios explore what happens when brand strategy is tested under different future conditions and what it might take to stay relevant, useful, and alive.

From the eight macro-forces (and their component drivers) several critical certainties emerged that will shape any future scenario:

- **AI-enhanced personalization** will become baseline infrastructure, intermediating attention and choice.

- **Fragmented identity ecosystems** will require brands to operate across multiple, shifting expressions of "self."

- **Experience-centric value creation** will remain a durable differentiator, particularly in physical and hybrid contexts.

At the same time, critical uncertainties were identified that could unfold in different directions:

- **Degree of consumer control** — whether people will assert sovereignty over data, visibility, and choice, or default to algorithmic convenience.

- **Centralized vs. decentralized brand shaping** — whether brands maintain control or become decentralized through technology and people.

- **Symbolic vs. functional brand preference** — whether people continue valuing image and narrative, or shift toward functional benefits and relationships.

These uncertainties shaped our scenario framework and revealed the strategic tensions brands must navigate.

Defining the Scenario Framework

These scenarios are structured provocations—windows into discrete worlds shaped by the certainties we must plan around and the uncertainties we must navigate. They stretch the imagination without detaching from reality, grounded in known drivers but extrapolated into plausible futures.

The scenario spaces were framed using two intersecting dimensions, each anchored in the most pressing uncertainties from our analysis:

Y-Axis: Symbolic/Systemic
This dimension examines what a brand truly represents in a given context. Does its value come primarily from narrative, identity, and cultural signal (Symbolic)? Or does it operate more like a system that people live with and act through (Systemic)?

X-Axis: Passive/Participatory
This dimension defines how people interact with a brand. Are they receivers of brand meaning, guided by top-down messaging (Passive)? Or

are they co-authors, shapers, and actors within brand systems (Participatory)?

Together, these axes form a matrix that surfaces four distinct futures—each a world where Brand must operate differently, build trust differently, and create value through different modes.

Four Brand Futures

The four scenarios are not ideal worlds or warnings. They are not ranked, and none represent a "preferred" future. Each is designed to pressure-test what new imperatives emerge for Brand, whether enabling possibility holds up, and what can be learned about creating value across different worlds.

Brand Futures Scenarios (*Fig. 4*)		
	Passive	**Participatory**
Symbolic	**Narrative Economy** Brands compete on mood, story, and aesthetic. Meaning is algorithmically served but rarely co-created. People consume symbolic resonance passively and emotionally.	**Cultural Remix** Brand meaning is open-source. People actively reshape symbols, memes, and messages. Participation happens through cultural play and narrative reinterpretation.
Systemic	**Invisible Infrastructure** Brands are ambient systems. Value is delivered through seamless service, not story. People rely on them without noticing–until they break.	**Collaborative Systems** Brands operate as participatory platforms. People co-create offerings, shape governance, and share value. Identity emerges through system participation, not brand messaging.

Each scenario is structured consistently to allow comparative learning across strategic coordinates, context and conditions, brand behaviour, people's experience, business implications, and the tensions that make each world ultimately unstable.

We begin with the most familiar space, the Narrative Economy.

Narrative Economy

In the Narrative Economy, brands compete for emotional resonance in a saturated symbolic marketplace. Storytelling is the dominant form of value through ads, campaigns, identities, and aesthetics. People engage primarily by consuming stories, moods, and values. Meaning is produced at scale but rarely lived.

It's a world trained on emotional response. AI-enhanced personalisation delivers people exactly the symbolic content that fits their mood, context, or micro-identity. Identity is fractured across channels and moments. What you see—and how the brand appears—is shaped by who the algorithm thinks you are in that moment.

Most brand interactions are mediated, not direct. Platforms, not people, do the choosing. Brand feeds are curated, aestheticized, and emotionally calibrated, down to colour grade, typography, and tempo.

But this precision has a cost. Fatigue sets in. Cultural meaning collapses into short-term trend fluency. Legacy brands rely on nostalgia to remain recognizable. New brands often arrive as moods, not models—stylized before they are understood.

Communities form, but they are not empowered. Fandom operates as amplification, not participation. Community-powered commerce becomes community-powered distribution, with little ownership or reciprocal value. Participation looks like sharing, rather than shaping.

Context & Drivers
This world emerges from the exhaustion of the purpose era, the fragmentation of platforms, and the full maturation of the algorithmic attention economy. As platforms optimised for performance, brands optimised for symbolism—turning feeling into the product and aesthetic coherence into the deliverable.

Certainties: Personalisation is unavoidable. Platform curation dominates. Emotional engagement remains competitive, but fatigue accumulates. Brands still need symbolic meaning to be recognizable.

Uncertainties: Will people tolerate total symbolic saturation? Will AI-driven brand intimacy feel manipulative or welcomed? Will attention become unmonetisable as people tune out?

Brand Role & Behaviour

Brands act as meaning-makers—deploying polished stories, values, aesthetic systems, and emotionally resonant content. They behave like emotionally intelligent broadcasters, with power lying in their ability to signal meaning across fragmented contexts and align with aesthetic and mood-aligned influencers (both human and AI-generated).

Most focus on rapid symbolic adaptation, including seasonal narratives, topical campaigns, and brand-meme executions. Some function as aesthetic operating systems—flexible brand toolkits tailored for platform performance and served up dynamically. Others invest heavily in genre-specific entertainment production, becoming cultural producers rather than just cultural mimes. Some brands may generate more revenue from image IP and merchandise than from core products and services.

Key strategies:

- Licensing and brand collaborations become major revenue streams

- Aesthetic fragments and cultural borrowing drive relevance

- AI-curated brand personalities adapt offers, tone and style dynamically

- Execution becomes central: tone, taste, visual language must stay culturally calibrated

Legacy brands rely heavily on familiar symbols to maintain their visibility. New brands are often born via aesthetic memes or micro-cultural moments.

People's Role & Experience

People experience brands through emotionally curated feeds. They may see different versions of the same brand depending on their mood, the time of day, or the social context. Brand interactions create emotional reactions—watching, scrolling, reacting—as recognition without relationship. Identity is reflected back to them—mirrored, not shaped.

Brand discovery occurs through algorithmic content surfacing, rather than active seeking. Some people opt out entirely, choosing "brand silence" or seeking minimalist brands that resist narrative inflation. Others treat brand feeds as entertainment media, consuming content built to provoke, distract, or amuse rather than anchor identity.

Emotional resonance still matters, but fatigue is high and trust is thin. People become increasingly sophisticated at recognizing and filtering symbolic manipulation.

Business & Platform Implications

Success is measured by symbolic share of voice, predictive cultural resonance, and emotional velocity. Brands are judged not on what they are, but how well they perform meaning in a given moment.

Campaign thinking dominates. Influencer culture remains powerful but becomes increasingly extractive and transactional. Many brands outsource cultural relevance to third parties, including creators, meme accounts, cultural consultants, and brand stylists.

Power dynamics:

- Platforms control visibility, emotional relevance, and distribution logic

- Media publishers regain strategic leverage as trusted cultural filters and narrative curators

- Creators become brand executors and surrogates, not just endorsers

- Traditional media companies may regain power as brands struggle with coherence across platforms

Strategic Tensions

- This scenario is not stable. Its contradictions generate conditions for collapse:

- Narrative fatigue creates hunger for authentic connection and relief from emotional manipulation.

- Symbolic saturation drives renewed demand for functional utility.

- Passive exposure breeds desire for agency and authorship—people want to shape, not just consume.

- Platform dependency creates vulnerability when algorithms change or platforms fragment further.

Early Signals

- Duolingo's owl persona becoming a cultural meme across TikTok and Twitter

- Ryanair's cynically self-aware social media voice gaining millions of followers

- MSCHF creating "vibe" products that prioritize cultural moments over utility

- Liquid Death turning water into a punk rock aesthetic performance

- Y2K revival brands like Collina Strada and Sandy Liang mining nostalgic aesthetics

- AI-generated avatars like the one Ukraine created to represent itself

- Brand collaboration fatigue occurs as Nike x Off-White loses distinctiveness amid endless partnerships

Invisible Infrastructure

In this world, brands are experienced through seamless systems. They're ambient, functional, and mostly invisible—woven into everyday life like electricity or bandwidth. People don't think about them unless something breaks.

Here, brand equity is operational. The promise is performance, not personality. You know the brand works because the system just flows. Consumers don't follow brand feeds or engage in symbolic exchanges. Instead, they interact with AI agents, predictive environments, and embedded interfaces. The brand doesn't talk at you—it configures around you. Services anticipate need. Experiences adapt in real time. Value is automated.

This world removes emotional labour and cognitive overload. Personalization happens quietly, through frictionless, system-led intelligence. But in removing friction, it also removes feeling. Without a visible presence, brand identity fades into utility—preference blurs. Default settings, trusted ecosystems, and the absence of pain replace loyalty.

Brand becomes metadata—backend codebases, machine-readable entities, and value protocols embedded in service layers rather than outward-facing narratives. Machine logic, embedded trust, and invisible performance surface brand discoverability through messages.

Some brands adapt by disappearing well. Others dissolve completely, unnoticed until the service fails. The new metric is uninterrupted experience.

Context & Drivers

This future emerges from fatigue—emotional overload, content saturation, and symbolic distrust. As performance marketing fractured and personalization matured, brands shifted from pushing meaning to embedding value. The smart ones stopped talking and started working.

Consumers began to expect functional harmony, including predictive logistics, zero-friction user experience, and seamless handoffs between digital and physical channels. The best brands were the ones that made life feel simple, even if people couldn't name them.

The physical world doesn't disappear—it becomes an extension of system logic. Physical stores function as infrastructure nodes, not brand theatres. Retail spaces are designed for responsiveness, not storytelling. Brands are felt through coordination, not colour palettes, its aesthetics subdued.

Certainties: The rise of automation, ambient computing, machine-readable systems, and the demand for predictive infrastructure.

Uncertainties: Will people accept brands they never see? Will trust in automation hold when systems fail? Will utility alone build preference? How do brands become discoverable in invisible systems?

Brand Role & Behaviour
Brands operate like operating systems: invisible, predictive, adaptive. Their role is to manage experience, not express identity—strategic focus shifts from campaigns to configuration. A brand acts as metadata—tagging criteria that become prompts to the system, adapting to context and use case.

Communication happens through interface design, service logic, and systemic reliability rather than brand messaging. Some brands survive on default trust: embedded in devices, payments, transportation, and homes. Others become backend services, licensing their operational logic to other ecosystems.

Key strategies:

- Revenue models shift toward subscriptions, infrastructure licensing, API integrations, and embedded commerce

- Brand equity collapses into performance measured by responsiveness and harmony and technical trust

- Engineering, logistics, data integration, and latency become brand differentiators

- Customization becomes a requirement for products and services

Symbolic assets lose strategic value unless they signal reliability or support lifestyle integration.

People's Role & Experience
People are users, not audiences. They experience brands ambiently—through interactions, not awareness. Brand choice often disappears: systems choose on their behalf. The absence of friction, not the presence of meaning defines success.

Discovery is backend-driven: AI agents or ambient systems match offerings to behaviour, context, and history. What once felt like loyalty becomes efficiency—brands are chosen for performance, not message. In some ecosystems, users manage visibility through self-sovereign data preferences, controlling what systems can surface based on mood, values, ethics, and attributes.

The physical world remains present, but it has been restructured. You might visit a store, but the product was pre-matched, and the checkout was invisible. Physical brand interaction becomes another system touchpoint: functional, fast, invisible by design.

But not everyone opts in. Some reject invisibility, worried about control, erasure, or the opacity of algorithms. Others demand "slower" modes—brands that ask before acting and provide transparent recommendation and curation processes.

Business & Platform Implications
Performance becomes the value proposition. Brands are judged by responsiveness, uptime, and harmony—not emotion or narrative. Orchestration creates brand-building.

Power dynamics:

- Infrastructure owners and integrators dominate (Amazon, Google, Shopify, Stripe)

- Platforms consolidate, owning infrastructure layers while outsourcing identity

- Consumers cede decision-making to systems in exchange for

ease

- Creators have limited relevance—no meaning layer to amplify

The most trusted brands may be the least visible. Brand valuation shifts from awareness to system utility, engagement architecture, and integration capability.

Strategic Tensions
Invisibility delivers utility but erodes identity. Over time, brands that optimise for seamlessness risk becoming interchangeable, even forgettable.

Distinction decays. If all systems work similarly well, why choose one over another? People begin to miss the presence, tone, and feelings over the features.

Failure becomes catastrophic. A single outage, data breach, or system failure can trigger massive distrust because the brand has no symbolic goodwill to buffer disruption.

Loss of agency accumulates as consumers notice they didn't choose anything—the system decided. Backlash grows through manual overrides, offline buying, a demand for slower modes, and more collaborative interfaces as people try to reestablish their bearings.

Early Signals

- Amazon's Alexa making purchase decisions through "best match" algorithms

- Smart home systems automatically reordering supplies

- Stripe processes payments where the brand appears only on receipts

- Apple Pay enables frictionless transactions and self-checkout

- Automotive platforms' white-labelling services, like GM's OnStar, are integrating multiple invisible providers

Cultural Re-mix

In the Cultural Re-mix world, brand meaning is no longer authored—it's co-authored. People don't consume brand stories—they rewrite them, mash them up, and feed them back into culture and brands. Identity becomes a participatory act. Symbolism is fluid, negotiated, unstable, and alive.

This world is loud, fast, and full of creative tension. Brand becomes raw material, not a finished product. Aesthetic fragments, memes, rituals, and inside jokes are constantly recontextualized across networks and subcultures. What a brand means depends on who is using it and in what context.

Here, value is about identity, emotion, and personal expression—but created from the bottom up. Brands survive by inviting reinterpretation in different formats for co-creation. The best brands don't protect their meaning—they open-source it. But not every brand is remix-worthy. This world exposes the fragility of symbolic equity of brands as only cultural objects. Brands that overestimate their cultural relevance may find their gestures ignored.

Remix lives in the symbolic layer. People don't remix product or service mechanics—they remix meaning. The brand's work is to make its aesthetic, tone, and narrative structure remixable. Participation is cultural, not functional.

Context & Drivers
Cultural Remix arises from the exhaustion of top-down meaning and mistrust of static brand identity. As younger generations grew up remixing memes, aesthetics, and narratives, they demanded that brands do the same. Authenticity no longer means fixed values—it means openness to reinterpretation.

AI tools, content templates, and modular brand assets made remix accessible to everyone. People started using brands like media, not just consuming them, but adapting them for personal expression, social signalling, and shared play.

Certainties: Persistent platform culture, symbolic saturation, demand for identity expression, AI-enabled creation tools.

Uncertainties: How much control will brands surrender? Will participatory creativity drive cohesion or fragmentation? Do most brands have enough cultural significance to sustain remix? How does cultural participation translate to business value?

Brand Role & Behaviour

Brands provide symbolic IP and remixable assets—taglines, visuals, audio, rituals, style systems. Meaning is created in the wild. Control is minimal. Curation happens after the fact, not before.

Strategic focus shifts to enablement, fluency, and elasticity—less about owning the message, more about enabling narrative flexibility. Legacy brands must unlearn control; emerging brands often skip formal identity entirely, starting as cultural toolkits.

Key strategies:

- Revenue through co-branded drops, cultural licensing, IP frameworks, and symbolic micro-commerce

- Value found in circulation, not coherence—but circulation doesn't guarantee returns

- Some brands adopt game-like logic, building symbolic universes that evolve through community, fan and guest contributions

- The brand becomes less of a statement and more of an ongoing story engine

Remix is high-stakes. Opening your brand to participation assumes that people find it culturally useful. Many brands invest considerable energy in symbolic toolkits that go unused, or worse prove culturally irrelevant. Others get absorbed and reshaped into meanings they can't control, losing coherence entirely.

People's Role & Experience

People are cultural producers. They shape, share, and recast brand meaning in service of personal expression. A product or symbol is only as powerful as its remix-ability. Identity is constructed through symbolic agency—choosing, altering, and deploying brand signals as a form of social performance.

The brand's meaning becomes whatever the community makes of it. People expect brands to be listening, adapting, sometimes just getting out of the way. Remix isn't entertainment—it's self-definition. People use brands to experiment with belonging, signal subculture, and co-create meaning in a chaotic symbolic landscape.

Key dynamics:

- Consumption becomes part of a continuous feedback loop

- Co-design, remixing, and brand extension become standard expectations

- Communities form around shared codes, cultural references, and inside language rather than ownership

- Belonging is performed through interaction, creation, and commentary as much as acquisition

Business & Platform Implications
Brand strategy becomes cultural choreography—orchestrating fluid meaning across unstable networks. Success is measured by participation volume, remix velocity, and cultural traction rather than traditional sentiment analysis.

Merchandising becomes the primary economic path—brands monetize symbolic relevance through limited drops, meme artifacts, fan-designed capsules, and aesthetic collectibles. Platforms surface brand creativity, making remix stats more important than reach metrics.

Power dynamics:

- Cultural communities hold symbolic power, creating multiple modes of expression

- Platforms algorithmically gate visibility, but people gate meaning

- Brands become stewards and incubators, not architects

- Creators become curators, translators, and amplifiers—less endorsement, more adaptation

- Media publishers regain relevance as cultural remix platforms, hosting brand extensions and co-authored content

Moderation and community curation become strategic disciplines as brands navigate the delicate balance between enabling participation and maintaining coherence.

Strategic Tensions
Remix is participatory but unstable. The line between cultural legitimacy and brand dilution is razor thin.

Too much openness risks coherence collapse. What if a brand means everything, everywhere? How do you maintain any strategic direction?

Not enough participation breeds irrelevance. If people can't remix, they ignore. But not all brands have sufficient cultural weight to sustain interest.

Ownership becomes contentious. Who owns a meme? A reskinned logo? A community redefinition? Legal and cultural boundaries blur.

Cultural legitimacy doesn't guarantee business value. Brands may find their identity everywhere, but conversion is nowhere to be seen. High engagement doesn't automatically translate to revenue.

The more you enable meaning, the less you control it. Brands risk being remixed into contexts that contradict their intended values or business objectives.

Early Signals

- Roblox users creating branded virtual worlds like Vans World that become fan-driven experiences

- IKEA's instruction manual memes, product hacks, and blue bag upcycles

- Duolingo fandom creating unofficial content shaping brand perception

- Supreme's box logo becoming raw material for countless streetwear remixes

- TikTok users remixing brand jingles and slogans into viral formats

- Nike's "Just Do It" being recontextualized across infinite contexts by communities

- Brands like Golf Wang releasing modular design assets for fan customization

Collaborative Systems

In this world, brands aren't stories or services—they are systems people participate in. Not just symbolically, but operationally. Value emerges from co-creation, shared governance, and systemic transparency.

This modular world emphasizes adaptive infrastructure and interdependent ecosystems. Brands behave less like companies and more like protocols—tools people build on, plug into, or adapt. The most successful brands don't launch campaigns—they invite integration.

People don't just buy into brands—they help steer them. From product logic to distribution models, feedback loops are continuous. Community isn't a marketing tactic—it's a structural component of how the brand operates and creates value, often functioning in semi-autonomous ways across the broader ecosystem.

Trust is systemic, not emotive. Co-design replaces brand promise. Participation becomes a form of ownership—even if not financial. The brand is what it enables, not what it expresses.

Context & Drivers

This future emerges from the breakdown of both symbolic authority and system opacity. As institutions faltered and brand stories eroded, people demanded the opportunity to help build the systems that impact their lives. Enabled by decentralized technology, modular interfaces, and open frameworks, brands evolved from fixed expressions into adaptive ecosystems.

Rising expectations for transparency, self-determination, and meaningful participation in the value creation process drove the shift. People wanted more than just a choice—they wanted a voice in how systems worked.

Certainties: Increasing demand for transparency, self-determination, customized products and experiences, and meaningful participation in value creation.

Uncertainties: Will people take responsibility for co-created systems? Can modular brands maintain coherence and trust at scale? How much control do people actually want in practice? Which categories and business models can realistically operate this way?

Brand Role & Behaviour

Brands behave like open platforms or living toolkits—not fixed identities. Focus shifts to governance models, system logic, value protocols, and interoperability. Brand equity becomes design equity: the clarity, flexibility, and power of the system itself.

Strategy becomes systems architecture: what can this brand enable others to do, be, achieve? Some brands offer APIs or design standards for co-creation and collaboration. Others allow communities to shape product direction, policies, or resource allocation. Consistency is maintained through clear logic and shared principles rather than rigid messaging.

Key strategies:

- Revenue generated through usage, tiered access, co-owned IP, and community-distributed returns (like dividends)

- Governance frameworks become brand differentiators, focused on outcomes

- Legal, design, and business models evolve to accommodate distributed participation

- Brand extensions emerge from the edge, not the centre

- Products and services become a collaborative infrastructure, not fixed offerings

The model leans toward reciprocal value, rather than one-way extraction. Brands may become embedded within communities, cities, or ecosystems as co-designed frameworks, rather than external entities.

People's Role & Experience
People are system actors—not just users, but contributors. Participation influences experiences, roadmaps, and trade-offs. Identity is built through participation: this is the system I help shape.

Brand loyalty is rooted in structural agency, not emotional affinity. This world asks more from people, but gives more in return. Ownership is cultural, behavioural, and systemic. Not everyone participates deeply, but everyone benefits from the logic of openness.

Key dynamics:

- People expect seamless transitions between contexts and roles within the system

- Feedback loops are continuous and visible

- Participation creates both rights and responsibilities

- Value creation is transparent and often shared

- Decision-making processes are accessible and inclusive

Business & Platform Implications
Platform thinking becomes operational reality: brands design for adaptability, not messaging. Brand valuation shifts from visibility to system utility, engagement architecture, and contribution flow.

Legal, design, and governance models must evolve to accommodate distributed participation. Success is measured through outcomes, including system health, contributor satisfaction, and collective value creation, rather than traditional metrics.

Power dynamics:

- Governance frameworks become competitive advantages

- Power flows through system design, not executive leadership or media presence

- People who shape the system can also shape the brand

- Media publishers become ecosystem collaborators, facilitating participation and co-creation rather than broadcasting messages

Brand breakdown occurs when governance fails, when participation becomes extractive, or when systems become too complex to navigate.

Strategic Tensions

Governance complexity increases with scale. As brand ecosystems expand across categories, contributors, and use cases, maintaining coherence becomes exponentially more difficult. What defines the core when the edges keep stretching?

Value equity becomes complex. Who benefits, and how fairly? As more people contribute, determining fair distribution of value—whether economic, social, or cultural—becomes contentious.

Participation vs. labour boundaries blur. Are people participating meaningfully, or working for free? The line between community engagement and unpaid labour becomes increasingly problematic.

Too much openness risks governance paralysis. When everyone has input, decision-making can become impossibly slow; too little risk can betray the participatory promise.

Coherence vs. flexibility tensions. How do you maintain integrity while enabling co-creation? Systems must be stable enough to function but flexible enough to evolve.

Scalability challenges. Participatory systems that work at a small scale may break down when they grow. Intimacy and agency become harder to maintain with size.

Early Signals

- Yvon Chouinard transferred ownership to environmental causes, creating a form of collective stewardship

- Nike's RTFKT/Nike Digital - using blockchain for digital sneaker ownership and authenticity verification

- Ben & Jerry's employees can earn equity through profit-sharing programs

- Discord communities co-creating brand roadmaps and product features

- Linux Foundation's collaborative governance model inspiring brand partnerships

- Fair Trade certification evolving into community-overseen brand standards

The Pattern in the Breakdown
Each scenario reveals the active tensions we're already living through.

Whether symbolic or systemic, passive or participatory, these divergent worlds expose a shared strategic breakdown: traditional brand approaches reach failure points when they optimise for single dimensions of value.

The Failure of Pure Approaches
Each scenario demonstrates the unsustainability of one-dimensional strategies:

- **Narrative Economy** shows how symbolic competition leads to saturation, fatigue, and algorithmic dependence. When brands compete only on meaning—without functional relevance—they become interchangeable entertainment.

- **Invisible Infrastructure** reveals how functional systems without emotional or cultural meaning create trust gaps. When everything works but nothing feels like anything, people begin to question what's been lost.

- **Cultural Remix** shows how participation without real outcomes becomes spectacle. Symbolic interaction only works for culturally dominant brands—and even then, it can collapse into superficial play.

- **Collaborative Systems** demonstrate that even participatory brands fail without structure, coherence, and fair value exchange. When contribution becomes invisible labour, trust collapses.

Shared Vulnerability

Across all four worlds, one pattern repeats: brands that optimise for a single mode of value become unstable.

They work until they don't.
They scale until they break.
They engage until people opt out.

These tensions point to a necessary evolution: brands that thrive will connect meaning with function, structure with agency, and symbolism with systemic capability. But connection takes more than intention. It calls for new strategic foundations—built for complexity, adaptability, coherence, and for enabling possibility.

The following chapter offers additional insight into what the era of possibility, the macro-drivers and these scenarios tell us about where brand strategy needs to build from.

make it your OWN

"Making it your own" captures something fundamental about how we connect to what matters.

It's the café where the barista knows your order. A tool shaped to your workflow. A community you've helped build. Something shared becomes personal—and more valuable because you've shaped it.

That's the essence of inhabiting a brand—not just consuming it.

For decades, brands have presented a false choice between personal relevance and collective belonging. Mass marketing offered neither. Personalization isolated. Community branding flattened individuality.

Making it your own dissolves that tension by letting you personalize something collective—adapting shared elements to fit your needs while staying connected to the whole. It enables individual expression within shared context—a way to shape something without owning it and belong without conforming.

The most future-fit brands aren't just open to being shaped by people—they're built for it. They enable different levels of participation: remixable brand elements, identity integration and enhancements, or co-evolution systems that grow stronger through use.

It isn't about pushing meaning out but inviting people in: How do people make your brand their own? What can be adapted without losing coherence? How does individual utility strengthen collective value?

The goal goes beyond mass customization—it's systemic enablement.

It doesn't mean brands stop selling. But in a world where products can be copied and attention is scarce, what people make of your brand—how they shape it, use it, extend it—is what makes it matter. Because helping people do something meaningful is the difference between having customers and cultivating inhabitants.

when brand becomes infrastructure

Dynamic futures require dynamic strategies. Strategies that are holistic, interconnected, and structurally adaptive.

The scenarios explored in the previous chapter weren't predictions. They were pressure tests. Each one exposed the conditions, tensions, and trade-offs brand strategy will need to navigate. Each one made visible the fault lines where existing brand approaches collapse: and the capabilities that must be present for new ones to thrive.

Despite their divergence, the scenarios echoed fundamental tensions:

- Symbolic competition is empty without functional relevance.

- Functional systems are empty without meaning.

- Participation without outcomes leads to fatigue.

- Infrastructure without meaning can't create cultural weight.

- Systemic co-creation requires shared value and clarity.

Each scenario's failure mode reinforced that brands must connect meaning and function to reach their full potential.

No scenario succeeded through pure approaches. Meaning alone faltered. Function alone broke. Brands need symbolism and systems, structure and agency, coherence and fluidity.

Interconnectedness is a structural requirement. It demands new foundations: models designed for complexity, elasticity, and the expanded role brands must now play across systems, cultures, and value networks.

The "To What End?" Test
The scenarios also revealed a single question underlying every strategy choice:

"To what end does our brand strategy enable possibility?"

Strategies that create engagement but don't build capability are fragile.
Efficiency without human agency invites resistance.
Participation without outcomes feels extractive.

The question isn't rhetorical: it's functional. If a strategy doesn't expand what people or businesses can do, it isn't built to last.

From Attention to Capability
One of the clearest shifts across the scenario exploration was this:

We're shifting from a brand era rooted in attention—measured in reach, relevance, and recall—to one defined by capability (measured in what people can do, solve, or become). Brands that thrive in this shift won't just capture attention. They'll expand capacity—for users, communities, and the systems they move through.

They will:

- Build tools that help people shape their own stories

- Shift from audience-building to ecosystem participation

- Move from owning narratives to co-creating shared logic

This isn't a departure from business value. It's an evolution of how brands now *create* it.

The Four Modes of Brand Enablement
Through the lens of these scenarios, and the structural forces shaping the era of possibility, four essential modes of enablement emerged. These modes are not optional. They form the strategic infrastructure that allows brands to function across change, enable others, and remain whole under pressure.

1. **Brand as Interface**
   The connective layer that makes systems accessible and inter-active. It enables people to see, understand, and act—making participation intuitive, navigation meaningful, and system engagement possible.

2. **Brand as IP**
   The symbolic and functional signature—the design, logic, or cultural assets that make the brand ownable and recognizable. This includes aesthetic identity, product "recipes", narrative frameworks, and experiential blueprints. It's what makes the brand recognizable and reproducible across contexts.

3. **Brand as Capability**
   What people can do, solve, or become as a result of the brand—tools, skills, confidence, access, or community that expand capacity.

4. **Brand as Protocol**
   The logic and behaviour that ensures coherence across changing conditions. It defines rules, standards, and permissions—how the brand adapts while staying whole.

These modes are interdependent. No single one is sufficient.
Brands will activate them in different configurations depending on context, strategy, and intent.

But the futures we explored were clear:

- An Interface without a Protocol leads to an inconsistent experience

- IP without Capability becomes ownable but not useful

- Capability without Interface is powerful but inaccessible

- Protocol without IP is systematic but forgettable

Together, these modes *are* brand infrastructure, allowing a brand to function as a system and through business design.

Commerce Remains. Consumption Evolves.
This shift toward enablement doesn't abandon commerce—it redefines how value is created, captured, and exchanged. People will still buy things. But their expectations are shifting:

- From extraction to enablement

- From ownership to access

- From transaction to participation

The definition of value now includes not just product or service, but the infrastructure, agency, and possibility that surround it.

Enablement Isn't Idealism
This isn't virtue-signalling in a new costume. *Enabling possibility* is not brand purpose. It's a strategic response to real complexity—to more distributed expectations, fluid markets, participatory systems, and adaptive infrastructures.

To enable possibility is to build systems that make things possible—at personal, collective, and systemic levels.

It shows up in:

- Entertainment that sparks self-expression

- Tools that remove barriers

- Systems that offer agency

- Experiences that combine meaning and utility

Enablement isn't aspiration. It's a design imperative.

Strategic Necessity
The Era of Possibility reveals more than shifting trends—it signals a deeper recalibration of value, meaning, and participation. Consumer trust is eroding, extractive models are breaking down, and the role of brand is expanding beyond narrative or image. Across divergent scenarios, one pattern held: only integrated strategies—those that combined

meaning with function, structure and capability, coherence and adapt-ability—proved future-ready. These aren't aspirational ideas. They are structural requirements. And they call for a new understanding of what Brand must now enable.

The structural requirements are clear. The model designed that follows is built to meet them—a new centre of gravity for Brand that con-nects meaning and function through the Brand Operating Idea, enabling brands to scale and stretch across systems, time, and use cases.

The Four Modes of Brand Enablement (*Fig. 5*)		
Enablement Mode	What It Is	Examples
Brand as Interface	The connective layer that makes systems, technologies, or processes intuitive and accessible to humans. Enables navigation, interaction, and participation.	UX/UI, branded AI agents, onboarding flows, physical store navigation, participation prompts, interaction rituals
Brand as IP	The brand's symbolic and functional signature–what can be recognized, reproduced, adapted, or remixed. Includes both aesthetic and structural elements.	Visual systems, sonic branding, product formulas, design systems, narrative templates, APIs, aesthetic codes
Brand as Capability	The capacity the brand builds in others–what people can do, solve, create, or access through the brand is practical empowerment, not just symbolic association.	Learning tools, creator platforms, co-design kits, communities of practice, access pathways, branded utilities
Brand as Protocol	The embedded rules and logic that shape how the brand behaves–what it permits, governs, or standardizes. Enables consistency across complexity.	Governance models, community standards, design guardrails, API permissions, tone logic, and modular interaction rules

How we stand out > What we stand for > Why we exist > How we exist

Enablement in an Era of Possibility

Meaningful Enhancement (Agency & Meaning)	Generative (2025+) *(Collaborative & Interdependent)*	Brand Enablement (Navigation & Participation)
Meaningful Consumer (and fractured participant)	*Systemic Disruption (2015-2023): Platform capitalism, AI rise, identity crisis, economic contradictions*	Brand Purpose & Ecosystems
The Social Consumer	*Digital Proliferation (2000s-2010s): Internet, UX revolution, social media, e-commerce*	Brand Image & Relationships
The Lifestyle Buyer	*Globalization (1980s-1990s): Deregulation, multinational scale, finance efficiencies, supply chains*	Brand Image & Equity Systems
The Mass Consumer	*Mass Media Era (1950s-1970s): TV, suburban growth, psychology in marketing, affluence*	Brand Positioning
Habitual product consumer	*Mass Production (1920s-1940s): Assembly lines, national markets, radio, early consumerism*	Brand Management & USP
Safety & Trust	*Industrialization (1800s-1910s): Mechanization, railways, urbanization, mass packaging*	Brand Marks
INDIVIDUAL	**COMMERCIAL ERA**	**CORPORATE**

Laddering the Shift: Brand, Economy, and the Individual (*Fig. 6*):
This table maps the parallel evolution of individuals, commercial eras, and corporate brand strategy—from industrialization to the emerging generative economy. Each row represents a rung in the strategic ladder, tracing how trust, identity, and meaning have shaped what people seek and how organizations respond. The top row signals a convergence: an era defined not by what brands say or sell, but by how they enable meaningful participation in the systems we live through.

3

Inhabit Brand

building for what's next

Section three introduces the strategic foundation needed to move from foresight to implementation. It outlines how systems thinking, futures orientation, and business design converge in the Inhabit Brand model and its core construct, the Brand Operating Idea (BOI)—the structure that enables brand strategy to function in dynamic environments.

Much of this book has centred on people—their expectations, identities, behaviours, and systems of meaning. What follows is not a departure from business logic, but a demonstration of how meaning and function integrate systemically. Most brand strategies fail because they treat them as separate rather than interdependent forces of value creation.

The shift is both external and internal. Externally, people still want to buy things—they just want things that also enable movement, creativity, belonging, or capability. Value now includes the infrastructure and experience surrounding products, not just the products themselves.

Internally, brand must become operational logic—a shortcut to clarity, alignment, and action that equips organisations to move, adapt, and generate new value. Possibility translates to capacity. Enablement becomes capability.

The following chapters outline the new foundations that are needed for brand strategy to achieve its full potential.

new foundations

Brand has long operated as an applied discipline. Its strength comes from its ability to integrate ideas from across domains—marketing, economics, design, social sciences—and translate them into strategies that work in context. That flexibility and synthesis are what have made brand strategy so enduring.

But, as the world becomes more interconnected, adaptive, and systems-focused, the disciplines applied to brand strategy must also evolve. Strategy now needs to hold greater complexity and offer more operational coherence.

Too often, organisations default to 'uncertainty' as an explanation for strategic paralysis. But uncertainty is frequently just complexity we haven't bothered to understand. We tend to frame uncertainty as the opposite of predictability, when in reality it's the expression of dynamics between systems and elements we haven't fully mapped. What looks like uncertainty is often the interplay of interdependencies, feedback loops, and emergent drivers. Similarly, *resilience* has become a strategic buzzword, but it often implies a return to a previous state—as if stability were the end goal. What brands need is adaptive capacity: the ability to live within complexity, respond to shifting dynamics, and keep creating value as systems evolve.

To meet that demand, brands need new foundations that bring together systems thinking, futures, and business design—disciplines that allow strategy to stretch, anchor, and function across the full spectrum of the business.

These are the underpinnings that enable brands to navigate today's complexity. Each discipline brings a distinct but complementary capability to brand strategy.

Systems Thinking

Systems thinking transforms Brand from signal to structure. It reveals the interconnectedness between the systems that influence people and business—systems in which both meaning and function coexist. Rather than treating product development, supply chains, and customer behaviour as separate variables, this approach exposes the hidden relationships that make or break brand strategy: how procurement decisions can undermine a sustainability campaign, or how employee experience directly shapes customer perception.

Most importantly, it identifies leverage points where brand interventions create disproportionate impact. These interventions open up new possibilities across the entire system. A brand becomes an active, interconnected system—and its strategy can accommodate complexity and guide us to new possibilities.

Futures Thinking

Futures thinking shifts brand strategy from reactive to anticipatory. Instead of chasing trends or optimising for current conditions, it explores multiple plausible futures to stress-test strategic choices. This isn't about prediction—it's about building adaptive capacity.

By understanding how macro-drivers could reshape the landscape, brands can design for emerging contexts rather than just existing markets. The result is strategy with stretch: coherent enough to hold direction, flexible enough to evolve as conditions change. A brand becomes infrastructure for future possibilities—not just a response to present realities.

Business Design

Business design grounds brand strategy in operational reality. It ensures brand meaning is embedded in the mechanics of value creation—how products are built, services delivered, and customer relationships structured. This discipline closes the dangerous gap between brand strategy and business practice.

Instead of floating above operations as inspirational messaging, brand strategy becomes integral to business model innovation, organisational design, and capability development. It governs how the business creates value and enables greater ecosystem coherence, making it easier to manage brands, not harder.

The Transformation
Together, these disciplines do more than support Brand—they transform its role and give companies more leverage. They allow brand strategy to shift from surface expression to structural intelligence. They move it from narrative to navigation. And they provide the logic necessary for a new kind of brand model to emerge: one that doesn't just describe what a brand is, but defines how it enables, evolves, and creates value.

The fundamental challenge with brand strategy today isn't that it has become irrelevant—it's that it operates with yesterday's logic. We need to design forward with new foundations, processes, and frameworks that lean into complexity because it's the only way to move past uncertainty.

Inhabit Brand and its Brand Operating Idea (BOI) provide that model. They allow brand strategy to inhabit the system, not just describe it. And in doing so, Brand is reclaimed as a business driver—not just a story to tell, but a structure to build from.

inhabiting brand

Brand is no longer what you stand for—it's what you inhabit.

That idea sits at the heart of this model and this book. It reframes Brand from something static and symbolic to something alive, embedded, and operational. It positions brands as something that must be inhabited by the business, by people, by systems, and by the value it creates in the world.

This chapter introduces the Inhabit Model—the strategic structure that helps brands move beyond outdated thinking and toward more adaptive, generative strategy. It outlines the core components of the model, shows how they connect, and offers practical guidance on working with them.

At the centre of this model sits one essential question: **"How can we enable possibility for people?"**

From foresight to function, this question is the organizing force behind the Inhabit approach. It shifts focus from belief statements, purpose declarations, and static positioning toward something brands can inhabit. It centres the brand on how it exists—what it makes possible in real, functional, and meaningful ways.

The question is expansive but grounded. It invites systems thinking. It drives action. It embeds meaning into the operations, services, products, and experiences that connect with people's lives. It moves the conversation from storytelling to system-building.

The question has scope: it applies across categories.
It has depth: it surfaces new meaning and operational pathways.
It has focus: it leads to coherent strategies for value creation.

While this question is central, it's not the only one. The model is intentionally question-driven. Evolving a brand's strategy—and more importantly, its structure—requires better questions at every level. Questions surface assumptions. They disrupt defaults. They expose systems and open new ground.

We'll walk through the core components that bring this organizing question to life:

- **Possibility** – the aperture, motives and value creation spaces the brand seeks to shape

- **Enablement** – the means, structures, capabilities, and systems that make that possibility real

- **Outcomes** – the evidence of value created across people, business, and ecosystems

- **BOI** – the strategic logic and construct that holds it all together

This is how brands move from abstraction to action.

Core Concepts and Relationships

The Inhabit approach is built around four interrelated components. Each is distinct, but none stands alone. Together, they form brand strategy.

These components replace legacy staples like mission, vision, purpose, and promise—not because those ideas are inherently wrong, just insufficient for the complexity brands must now navigate.

At the heart of the model is a simple but powerful sequence:

- Possibility is the aperture.

- Enablement is the design direction.

- Outcomes are the evidence.

- The BOI is the conceptual structure that enables.

When Possibility and Enablement come together, they define the brand's role in enabling possibility—a foundation that becomes the core of the Brand Operating Idea and for delivering outcomes.

This chapter defines each component and explains how they interact to create a strategy for enabling value through systems thinking.

Possibility

Possibility defines the meaning space—the aperture for value creation—through the lens of people (me, we, us). It sets the stretch: what becomes possible when the brand is functioning at its best for people, for society, for systems.

> Uber disrupted taxi services by addressing a larger need: making on-demand access possible through mobility. That opened new value pathways beyond rides to food delivery, freight, and even flying cars.

It reframes how we define arenas. It moves us from fixed categories ("we're an automotive brand") to systems ("we're in the business of mobility").

Possibility is always framed outside-in—it begins with people, their context, and what they want to make possible in their lives.

Importantly, possibility is expansive but not limitless. Defining the arena sets boundaries for what value the brand can meaningfully and systemically create.

The key question—"How can we enable possibility for people?"—acts like the systems-futures version of "How Might We" framing, anchoring the work in real, emergent needs and conditions.

Enablement

If Possibility is the call, Enablement is the response. It defines how the brand creates the conditions for possibility to be realized. What role does the brand play in enabling what people want to do, solve, or become?

> *Shopify doesn't just enable e-commerce—it creates payment systems, marketing tools, and an entire small business ecosystem.*

Enablement integrates business-side inputs—capabilities and constraints, capacity limitations, and category dynamics—to inform what a brand can actually influence and activate. It maps new assets, potential partnerships, and identifies the brand's right to play or lead.

Enablement defines the brand's functional role. It connects the strategic opportunity to systems, operations, and people's real contexts.

Outcomes

Outcomes are the evidence of enabling possibility. They articulate the observable impact across people, business, and systems. They start directional, but over time must translate into concrete measures that shape decisions, design, and delivery.

> *Duolingo measures real-world language proficiency, time to fluency, and learning retention, not just app engagement.*

Strong strategies define outcomes across nested time horizons—near-term, mid-term, and long-term—to ensure traction and progress.

Brand Operating Idea (BOI)

The BOI is the conceptual and structural core of Inhabit Brand. It unites Possibility, Enablement, and Outcomes into one coherent, adaptive idea that operationalizes the brand across decisions, experiences, and behaviours.

Patagonia's BOI might be represented by: "enabling environmental activism through outdoor gear." It connects product durability, supply chain practices, and political advocacy into one strategic system.

The BOI is where strategy stops floating and starts functioning. It connects business systems and customer outcomes through brand logic. It enables people—and systems—to inhabit the brand in ways that are useful, participatory, and future-fit.

It's not a rejection of traditional brand strategy. It's a reclamation of its full potential: as business logic, as systems design, and as a force for coherence in complexity.

The Four Strategic Building Blocks (*Fig. 7*)		
Component	**Function**	**Focus**
Possibility (Who / Why)	Defines the aperture for value creation	Orients the brand toward people and systems, value creation and opportunity.
Enablement (How / What)	Defines the brand's role and functional logic	Shapes how the brand creates the conditions for value and action.
Outcomes (What / By When)	Provides evidence of real value and impact	Grounds the strategy across time horizons and systems in impact.
BOI (How We Exist)	Aligns and activates the system	Guides business design, decisions, and evolution as a coherent structure

Before a BOI can take shape, we need to identify the brand's value creation zone—the place where meaning and function most powerfully intersect through the lens of possibility.

Mapping the Value Creation Zone

The value creation zone is the strategic "sweet spot" where meaning and function converge. It's not just where the brand is relevant—it's where it can create value by intervening in the systems that brands and people interact through.

This zone acts as the connective tissue between Possibility and Enablement. It's where future opportunities meet the brand's ability to act, and it becomes the foundation for the Brand Operating Idea.

Arenas

Arenas matter because they create the right aperture — the balance of focus and expansiveness — to see where value can be created. They're not just a broader label for a category. In systems thinking, we're looking at many systems that intersect, overlap, and influence each other. An arena frames these interrelationships so you can map where meaning and function meet, where value flows, and where the brand can intervene. Categories can't do that — they trap you inside a single, narrow system.

> *Netflix moved from DVD rental to entertainment, opening space to become a streaming service, content creator, and global media platform.*

Every brand strategy exploration starts by defining the arena—the broad systems boundary within which value creation can happen. The arena creates boundaries that allow exploration of how different elements and systems interrelate rather than viewing them in isolation. The arena is not an end state or a target category. It's provides the context for dynamic systems (social, economic, political, environmental, etc.) within which brands and people coexist.

In traditional brand strategy, the process often starts with the business problem and category dynamics. But categories are narrow, backward-looking, and industry-centred. They tell us where the brand has been, not where it could go. This approach reinforces the status quo rather than generating new possibilities. And, bus ness problems, even if identified accurately, don't provide the space for sense-making.

For example:

- Instead of thinking "automotive," reframe the arena as mobility.

- Instead of "beauty," reframe it as expression or self-image.

These broader arenas enable help us frame the question: *"How can we enable possibility for people in this arena?"* The arena sets the system boundary for that question, creating the exploratory space where meaning and function intersect.

Meaning and Function Spaces

Through the process of exploration and sense-making—using systems mapping and futures inputs—you begin to arrive at a zone of value creation that's informed by how people relate to the arena and the elements within it. These zones define pathways of possibility: what people value, and where and how the brand can intervene. They also inform foresight scenarios used to understand the role the brand can play.

> *Airbnb's meaning space within the arena of belonging is authentic connection, while its functional space is local immersion.*

This approach draws from systems thinking—particularly the concept of stocks and flows—to understand how meaning, influence, and resources accumulate or deplete over time. Stocks represent what builds up—like trust, equity, or cultural relevance. Flows are the interactions, expressions, or decisions that feed or drain those stocks over time.

The value creation zone is made-up of two critical spaces:

- Meaning Spaces – emotional, cultural, symbolic dimensions: identity, motivation, values.

- Function Spaces – behavioural, technological, economic dimensions: access, tools, systems.

Together, they define the interdependencies and frictions where the brand can intervene and enable. They ensure that the strategy is both resonant and systemically grounded.

Reframing

Reframing is a core systems-thinking move (and within strategy generally). It shifts perspective. It moves strategy beyond defaults, categories, and inherited assumptions to open new strategic space.

When we reframe, we can ask better questions. We reveal new value flows. And we design strategies that are truly generative, not just iterative. Reframing helps us connect possibility and enablement strategically from past and present to future.

In a world of computers that ported business logic into the home, Apple reframed *personal computing* into *personal expression and creativity*. This shift expanded the arena from utility and productivity to identity and culture—opening entirely new value spaces in design, media, and lifestyle.

The Four Modes of Brand Enablement

We return briefly to the four modes of enablement (see Fig. 5). The four modes are as useful in early exploration as they are in late-stage BOI prototyping and business design definition.

These modes help brands expand value creation by allowing them to:

- audit where they have strengths and deficits, or see what's under-leveraged

- make decisions about what to prioritize and tap into

- understand what the different relationships exists between modes of enablement and futures scenarios

- understand which potential brand strategies and BOIs have the most viability or feasibility

By starting with mapping arena systems, meaning and system spaces, and applying modes of enablement, brands can build strong strategic scaffolding around meaning and function to create brand strategy that is fully operational.

The framework is nearly complete, but before mov ng forward, there's one last legacy construct to dismantle: vision. Not to separate it from outcomes, but to retire it entirely in favour of something more operational. In complexity, aspiration without enablement is theatre. Outcomes—nested across time horizons and grounded in the BOI—offer a more reliable organizing force for strategy, because they connect ambition directly to action.

outcomes over vision

While mission and vision have long guided strategy, vision has proven surprisingly resistant to scrutiny in both theory and prac-tice.

Vision once offered a picture of where companies aspired to go—meant to inspire and orient business direction. But in today's context, it often obscures more than it clarifies. Vision has become a placeholder: a lofty statement that sounds motivating but offers little practical traction. Even when purpose replaced mission, vision remained untouched—held up as a kind of strategic heirloom, carried forward without reevaluation.

But vision, as we've inherited it, is increasingly unfit for today's strategic demands. In a world shaped by complexity and speed, a singular future state no longer makes sense.

This is where outcomes come in.

A Shift in Focus
Outcomes aren't just a grounded version of vision, they mark a distinct strategic orientation.

Where vision looks forward, outcomes reach outward, focusing on the impact the Brand creates in the world rather than the state it wants to achieve. They don't define what the Brand intends to become—they define what the Brand makes possible.

This shift matters because strategy itself is being reframed. It's no longer enough to set direction; we must define impact. Outcomes provide a more tangible logic, allowing brands to define value as a consequence, not just an aspiration.

It's not a reduction. It's an expansion but with clear accountability.

Possibility and Outcomes
Rather than pinning brands to a single vision, brands should orient around possibility: the range of futures they can shape or participate in.

This connects directly to the Inhabit framework introduced in the previous chapter. Possibility gives us the stretch and permission to imagine more. Outcomes ground that potential in tangible, observable change.

What Outcomes Offer
Outcomes create coherence—not just across departments, but across contexts.
Unlike traditional vision statements, outcomes are dynamic. They evolve both within and outside the business.

They make success measurable across human and business dimensions, connect brand strategy directly to operations, allow brands to act across multiple time horizons, and avoid the trap of ambiguity (namely, interchangeability) that plagues mission, vision and purpose definitions in many organizations.

Outcomes don't declare value. They demonstrate it.

What Outcomes Look Like
For a digital healthcare platform: Achieve a 30% increase in patient adherence across chronic care plans within 18 months, while reducing clinical support costs by 20% through integrated self-management tools.

For a circular home goods brand: Shift 25% of purchases to refill formats within two years, reducing per-customer packaging waste by 60% and driving recurring revenue growth by 35%.

These examples connect measurable business results with meaningful human impact. They're defined results that can guide product teams, supply chain decisions, partnerships, and experience design much better than a vision statement.

Outcomes Aren't KPIs

It's essential to distinguish outcomes from KPIs (Key Performance Indicators) or OKRs (Objectives and Key Results).

- KPIs measure performance by tracking outputs—like engagement or conversion. They're helpful, but reactive. They tell you how you did, not what matters.

- OKRs are a strategic goal-setting framework. But in practice, they often devolve into departmental targets that lose their strategic connection.

Outcomes define what matters, making KPIs and OKRs more meaningful. They're inherently cross-system and focused on value creation, not just goal achievement.

They ensure that what's good for the business is also meaningful for people. Importantly, they also make a brand's value more tangible.

The Foundation of Strategic Action

Outcomes move us beyond vision—not because they discard aspiration, but because they give it consequence.

With enabling possibility as the driver, and outcomes as the measure of real-world impact, the BOI becomes the operational pulse of the brand. It replaces the fragmented legacy of mission, vision, and purpose with a single, adaptive structure—one that directs, aligns, and proves strategy in action.

With these foundations in place, we turn to the Brand Operating Idea.

the brand operating idea

Brand strategy, as we've inherited it, is full of good intentions but usually short on traction. Purpose statements signal intent but don't guide how a company behaves. Brand platforms win awards but fail to expand their value across the business. Strategies sound strategic—yet remain disconnected from what gets built, sold, or experienced.

And, it's the same pattern I kept seeing: strategy held back by linear internal processes, legacy frameworks, weak definition, lack of leadership investment, functional silos, and non-existent operational pathways.

Why the BOI Exists
I didn't set out to create a new model. I was simply tired—tired of watching good strategy go nowhere, and increasingly concerned about how "Brand" had lost its way inside organisations, out in the world, and as a discipline.

I wanted a model for brand strategy built to be inhabitable—because brand is no longer what you stand for; it's what you inhabit. The Brand Operating Idea was built to be just that.

It's the *how*—brand strategy expressed as a construct that makes meaning and function interoperable. Practical and actionable, yet filled with possibility, it works because it's built to be applied, not abstracted.

What the BOI is (and Isn't)
A BOI defines the strategic construct a brand inhabits to enable possibility—inside the business and out in the world.

It is not a description of brand intent. It is the operating logic. It lives at the intersection of what the brand makes possible for people, how the business enables that possibility, and what manifests across the system. It replaces the one-directional nature of purpose and positioning with something generative, adaptive, participatory, and operationally sound.

The BOI is built to work. It gives everyone—from the C-suite to functional teams—a clear understanding of the brand's role in value creation and how to enable it. Designed to guide business design, it doesn't get lost in translation.

The BOI is both a system and a construct for meaning-making: emergent and intentional, and strategic and sense-making.

That duality is essential. Strategy has to live, move, and expand. The BOI gives structure to that complexity while maintaining a singular, substantive strategic idea at its core.

The word "idea" might sound soft for something this foundational, but that's its strength. Strategy is about ideas. Most companies lack a strategy worth operationalising because they lack conceptual rigour. They have goals, aspirations, positioning statements—but not a strategic idea that can drive decisions, organise systems, scale or stretch.

If you don't have a core idea:

- What are you operationalising?

- What are you designing against?

- How are you innovating and adapting?

- What are you building value around?

The Four Qualities of a Strong BOI
The Brand Operating Idea defines how a brand inhabits the world in a way that creates value for people and the business—and becomes a structure others can inhabit in return.

A strong BOI is:

1. **Generative and Future-facing** - Opens new value creation capacity that can hold complexity.

2. **Coherent and Clear** - Aligns through one structural idea.

3. **Operational and Adaptive** - Evolves systems and connects strategy to implementation.

4. **Universal and Participatory** - Works across contexts and enables people in the system.

The Five Balances of The BOI
A strong BOI doesn't just define what the brand enables—it must sustain that strategic core over time, through change, and n the face of complexity.

To do that, the BOI must balance the key tensions every living system navigates. These Five Balances act as design tensions that keep the BOI coherent yet flexible—not overly rigid, but not so loose that it loses focus. They help teams evaluate whether the BOI has strategic desirability, operational viability, and long-term feasibility.

Think of them as the structural requirements that allow a BOI to stay dynamic. Without them, even the most compelling strategy will eventually become unstable or irrelevant as conditions shift.

It's these five balances in combination with a systems and futures development path that give the BOI a stable core and adaptive capacity. Unlike traditional positioning that defines what a brand is in fixed terms, the BOI is designed as a fixed idea with inherent adaptive capacity. This give brand strategy built-in flexibility to manifest differently across changing contexts and conditions.

The Brand Operating Idea isn't just a better way to articulate strategy, it's a more effective way to inhabit it.

In the coming chapters, we'll explore how this approach works in practice—examining real-world examples of brands that operate from this enabling logic, and outlining the process for developing and implementing your own BOI.

The Five Balances of the Brand Operating Idea (*Fig. 8*)		
Balance	**Does the BOI...**	**Watch Out For**
Meaning + Function	Connect symbolic value with practical utility and system logic?	Strategies that inspire but don't enable–or that function but don't resonate.
Flexibility + Coherence	Act as a stable core that enables diverse but consistent expressions?	Strategies that are too rigid (inhibiting adaptation) or too loose (causing fragmentation).
Domain-Specific + Arena Applicable	Hold relevance within a specific domain while applying across a broader arena of value creation?	Strategies that are so generic they lose distinctiveness–or so narrow they can't stretch.
Direction + Adaptation	Provide a clear strategic orientation while allowing contextual application and evolution?	Strategies that are aimless (no focus) or brittle (resistant to change).
Capability + Capacity	Connect to what the organization can currently deliver while creating space to grow what it can hold?	Strategies that overpromise (leading to disillusionment) or underdeliver (limiting impact).

brand is A PROMPT

We're entering an age of generative logic. In technology, prompts create outputs. Agents act on our behalf. Systems are no longer just reactive–they're co-creative.

But this isn't just a shift in how tech behaves. It's a shift in how we relate to systems altogether.

Brand belongs in this conversation–not as an artifact, but as a generative element.

A brand is a prompt: a designed input that triggers action, shapes direction, and generates value across a system. When designed well, it doesn't just communicate–it initiates. It doesn't just represent–it enables.

People are prompts, too. They signal needs, make choices, adapt behaviours, and remix meaning. They don't just respond to brands–they co-generate with them. They bring their context, agency, constraints, and imagination.

In this era, people are not passive endpoints of brand strategy or business models. They're agents in the system–co-designers, co-directors, co-builders of value.

This is the shift enablement demands. Brands don't generate value alone. They set conditions for value to emerge through participation, navigation, and mutual generativity.

This means developing brands as systemic prompts–inputs into experiences, decisions, behaviours, innovations, and culture.

A brand is not a position. It's a prompt. Not a belief. A generative structure. Not a performer. A participant.

To enable possibility, brands must become both prompt and interface. They must act–and allow others to act with them. Because in this new strategic system, people aren't your audience.

enabling possibility: in practice

Brands don't create value through what they say—they create value by what they make possible.

This section shows how the Inhabit Brand model reframes brand strategy by focusing on enabling possibility—unlocking outcomes that are both meaningful and functional for people and the business.

The following cases demonstrate how the approach enables brands to move beyond static purpose statements, helping them inhabit new roles and build coherent systems that generate new pathways of value and participation.

Loneliness: From Problem to Possibility

Many not-for-profit organisations express their intent through purpose statements such as: "We exist to end loneliness."

While well-meaning, this framing tends to lock organisations into problem-naming rather than solution-building. It creates a gap between intention and action—a space where many efforts default to awareness, fundraising, or advocacy without shifting systemic outcomes.

By asking, "How can we enable possibility for people?" we are asking a question of both meaning and functionality.

In this strategic demo of reframing purpose to enabling possibility, the arena that frames our problem and human experience is Connection. The meaning space that provides possibility is companionship—what people lack and seek when they experience loneliness. The system's space creates many pathways for intervention. In this case, the most accessible path for most people is shared interests—a system through which companionship can naturally form and expand. This results in: "We make it possible for people to find companionship by enabling connection through shared interests."

It's a simple yet powerful strategic reframe: shifting from naming a negative state to creating possibility. This reframe shifts the brand from intent to action, providing a clear value creation zone and strategy to guide further development. Importantly, it also makes it far easier to name outcomes and track impact, something that ultimately creates more support for the non-profit organisation because it has evidence to back up its cause.

Virgin: The Limits of Licensing Attitude

Before its time, Virgin looked like a brand becoming an ecosystem—but it lacked the structure to hold it together. In the early 2000s, Virgin seemed poised to be everywhere, for everyone: airlines, music, mobile, banking, health clubs, even cola and bridal wear.

But Virgin's business expansion was built on a shaky foundation. The brand's approach was rooted in attitude, not architecture. It projected a challenger spirit, but most of its growth came from licensing the name, rather than building shared systems or coherent operational models. Each Virgin business existed as a silo: loosely connected by tone, but rarely by any tangible system of value creation.

The result was the classic easy-money model—a surface-level growth strategy reliant on brand image rather than actual enablement. Virgin succeeded in creating an emotional signal (fun, anti-establishment, daring) but failed to build the functional infrastructure that makes a brand truly durable, participatory, and expansive.

Why the Four Modes of Enablement failed:

Over-reliance on IP: Virgin's core asset was its name and attitude, but without a unifying BOI or systemic logic, symbolic capital wasn't enough to stretch credibly across categories.

Lack of Capability: Virgin rarely enabled people to do, achieve, or become something new—extensions lacked depth or meaningful differentiation.

Fragmented Interface: Customer experience was inconsistent across businesses, with no shared brand architecture or ecosystem value.

Absent Protocol: Virgin never created clear systems for how people could participate, shape, or co-create within the brand.

As a result, Virgin's once-expansive reach has contracted. Many ventures have disappeared. What remains is a set of largely unrelated businesses trading on a fading brand mythos.

What Virgin Could Have Been: Had Virgin developed a coherent BOI around enabling the thrill of newness, discovery, and innovation ("virgin experiences"), it could have built something more generative. It would have provided a strategic core from airlines to fitness to entertainment, creating systems where people could try, test, and shape new experiences rather than consume Virgin's attitude (which amounted to a logo).

Red Bull: Immersive Systems

Red Bull offers a strong example of how a coherent BOI, anchored in systems and participation, can deliver long-term relevance. Rather than relying solely on messaging, Red Bull built meaning through action—creating immersive systems first and inhabiting cultural niches.

The core idea—"Gives You Wings"—functions as a proxy BOI: enabling people to push limits, unlock energy, and participate in peak experiences. The brand doesn't just tell a story—it creates the conditions for people to experience it.

Strong Foundation: Red Bull already excels across three enablement modes:

- Capability: Product performance and access to extreme sports and cultural platforms.

- IP: Distinctive codes, voice, and visual systems.

- Interface: Highly immersive events and branded experiences.

Together, these create a coherent Red Bull world. But there's room to stretch further.

The Growth Opportunity: Participation today is largely curated—Red Bull directs the experience. To evolve, the brand could shift toward deeper shared agency. This is where Protocol could open new pathways: systems that allow people to propose ideas, remix content, host local events, or contribute to the brand's evolution.

Strategic Risk: Growth pressures often push brands toward flattening their edge. For Red Bull, this might look like:

- Diluting meaning through low-stakes energy formats

- Over-extending into functional wellness trends

- Competing on flavour proliferation, not cultural impact

To avoid this, Red Bull must evolve from a performance brand into an agency brand—still about energy, but positioned around what people can achieve or influence, not just how hard they push. The brand is closer to Duracell than Energizer. It isn't just about endurance ("keeps going and going"). It's about potency, intensity, and being the energy you choose when it matters.

A Generative Path: One possible evolution lies in the cultural resurgence of DIY, punk, and protest. This isn't nostalgia—it's a response to disillusionment with broken systems: climate collapse, economic inequality, political distrust. Red Bull has always championed intensity—this could extend into the realm of grassroots creativity and movement-building.

Here, "Gives You Wings" becomes less about adrenaline and more about collective action: supporting micro-movements, enabling independent creators, and building local culture infrastructure.

This doesn't dilute the core idea. It expands it—applying Red Bull's energy ethos to a broader field of action, where people don't just consume intensity but co-create it.

Toyota: Reframing Automotive
For a Mobility Evolution

This speculative case shows how the Inhabit Brand method can reframe brand possibility—using systems-futures thinking to unlock new pathways for relevance and growth.

The automotive industry has become trapped in false binaries: electric versus combustion, ownership versus sharing, and driver versus self-driving. Most brands continue to obsess over the vehicle itself while missing profound cultural shifts that are reshaping how people think about movement, freedom, and home. This narrow framing has stalled genuine innovation, keeping design focused on technology and fuel sources rather than asking more profound questions about the role of mobility in people's lives.

When Moving Becomes Living. In the future where cars no longer require drivers, they cease to be "cars" in the traditional sense. They become hybrid spaces, extensions of home, work, and social environments, where life continues rather than pauses in motion.

Rather than competing to build the best electric or autonomous vehicle, Toyota could reframe its strategic role around this (speculative) BOI: "Autonomous Mobility Living". This idea shifts the focus from perfecting vehicles to enabling adaptive living—through seamless integration between mobility and broader life systems.

Signals of this shift are already emerging. In Japan and beyond, more people are embracing nomadic lifestyles—using vehicles as study zones, nap spaces, or temporary homes. As commutes evolve and transportation modes multiply, the concept of what constitutes a "car" is dissolving. People are integrating home into vehicle and vehicle into home, softening the boundary between mobility and habitation.

The real promise of Autonomous Mobility Living isn't automation—it's autonomy. The freedom to move, work, rest, and connect on your terms. Mobility systems that adapt to life, not the other way around. Autonomous Mobility Living isn't just about technology—it's about enabling people to move through life with greater ease, freedom, and peace of mind. It means never feeling disconnected from home, from community, or from what matters most—even when you're on the move.

Consider a morning where your commute becomes your mobile office, complete with the same lighting, temperature, and workspace configuration as your home. When you arrive at work, your vehicle seamlessly transfers stored energy to power the building while you're inside. When you return home, it docks with your house, extending your living space and contributing to your home's energy grid.

Philosophical and Capabilities Alignment: Toyota's existing capabilities make this speculative direction plausible and powerful. Its manufacturing excellence, hybrid innovations, energy R&D, and long-horizon projects like Woven City provide a credible foundation for this kind of systems-level evolution.

The BOI doesn't abandon Toyota's Kaizen heritage—it extends it into new territory. If Kaizen is about continuous, incremental improvement, Ma is about designing what connects—transitions, spaces, and the flow between. Together, they enable a richer kind of hybrid thinking. This shift reframes Toyota's role: not just perfecting the car, but orchestrating the flow between mobility, habitation, and energy.

This evolution extends Toyota's hybrid thinking from vehicles to "living hybrids"—systems that blend mobile and stationary experiences, individual and community energy, and private and shared spaces. This shift would elevate Toyota from a reliable product to a reliable infrastructure— becoming the foundational layer that enables autonomous living, rather than just another autonomous vehicle —and claim cultural and systems leadership. At the same time, competitors remain locked in hardware and software wars.

The Four Modes of Enablement:

- **IP enablement** means Toyota develops design language and integration standards around mobility docking—the seamless interface between moving and stationary life, anchored in the Japanese design principle of Ma. This cultural authenticity provides a position no competitor can easily copy.

- **Capability enablement** leverages Toyota's manufacturing excellence and hybrid expertise to create modular living components—interiors that reconfigure based on journey purpose, expanding into mobile offices, meditation spaces, or family entertainment centres.

- **Interface enablement** focuses on transition experiences—every moment when you move from home to vehicle must feel effortless and harmonious, creating a new standard for what mobility feels like and looks like.

- **Protocol enablement** creates open standards and community co-creation platforms that enable people to shape the evolution of their autonomous living systems, with communities collaborating on local infrastructure and configurations.

This reframes Toyota—not as a carmaker, but as an architect of autonomous living. A system builder, not just a vehicle maker.

Mike's Hard Lemonade:
Regenerating A Static Brand

Mike's Hard Lemonade offers a clear example of a stalled brand—trapped by a shallow category code ("hard") and lacking a system of enablement to evolve meaning or generate new value in a competitive, commoditized drinks category.

The (Working) BOI: Hard-core Mixers: The opportunity lies in redefining brand strategy. The BOI, "Hardcore Mixers", brings together drinks, people, and passions. This reframes Mike's as a brand that enables people to celebrate and share the things they go "all in" on—their fandoms, obsessions, hobbies, aesthetics, and social experiences.

Everyone is a little "hardcore" about something. The insight is grounded in the rise of niche lifestyle codes—such as grannycore, Y2K core, tomato girl summer, dark academia, and DIY culture—where people express their identity through deep immersion in their interests and latest obsessions.

Mike's can become the drink that mixes with whatever that "something" is—unlocking playful identity, creative expression, and social belonging. It's entirely generative.

Four Modes of Enablement:

- **IP enablement** fosters a remixable, open-source brand identity—creating symbolic assets and design codes people can use to express their passions. It unlocks dynamic innovation and fuels the other modes of enablement.

- **Capability enablement** empowers consumers to become creators through modular flavour concentrates tied to specific communities or aesthetics, plus DIY mixology tools that make customization easy using base formulas with Nespresso-like interfaces.

- **Interface enablement** creates pop-up experiences and digital activations that genuinely connect people around shared passions—authentic spaces where people live out their identities with pride.

- **Protocol enablement** introduces "Hardcore Certification" systems that allow superfans to contribute ideas, co-create limited editions, or host events within clear brand guidelines.

Anchored in the Hardcore Mixers BOI and activated through the four modes of enablement, Mike's can move beyond casual, transactional drinking to become a playful, expressive, and participatory brand—built for growth in today's fragmented, identity-driven culture.

Personal Injury Law:
From Legal Advocacy to Legal Care

This case draws on original thinking from a past client engagement—showing how BOI strategy can unlock value, even in unlikely categories.

Personal injury law has long been trapped in static positioning: "We stand up for you," "We fight for justice." While these convey strength, they offer little differentiation—or room for growth—in a category increasingly driven by volume and efficiency.

Meanwhile, macro forces are reshaping the landscape. The American way is increasingly precarious: no universal healthcare, unstable employment, failing institutions. People face growing vulnerability with decreasing protection. Insurance companies use data and complexity to marginalize claims while individuals struggle alone against extractive systems. Personal injury law is becoming increasingly complex and fluid, as it intersects with other legal practice areas and with expanding definitions of personal injury.

Law at the Centre of Quality of Life: When systems fail—which they increasingly do—legal expertise can shift from crisis response to a foundation for care.

Step away from incident reactivity, and new possibilities emerge: legal services could function as the organizing principle for integrated support. Just as concierge medicine reframed healthcare around whole-person wellness, legal services could evolve toward proactive care pathways—with PI law at the centre of quality-of-life outcomes.

The BOI, Whole-Person Legal Care, reframes legal expertise as the foundation for prevention, protection, recovery, and community resilience.

Legal expertise serves as the foundation for integrated care, encompassing the coordination of healthcare navigation, financial planning, workplace safety, emotional well-being, and community protection. Think of it as care meets blockchain: distributed but accountable, interconnected yet held to a legal standard—designed to strengthen both individuals and the communities they live in from accidents, identity theft, human trafficking and more. This model benefits from comprehensive care and improved outcomes, rather than relying on volume efficiencies at scale.

The Four Modes of Enablement:

- **IP enablement** defines the intellectual framework for whole-person legal care—standards, data, methodologies, and research that connect law to other life systems.

- **Capability enablement** builds tools and services—from community wellness hubs to digital platforms—that enable cross-disciplinary care and proactive community resilience.

- **Interface enablement** designs experiences that reinforce dignity, trust, and belonging. Every touchpoint supports not just service delivery, but prevention and recovery.

- **Protocol enablement** creates membership models and care standards that shift legal practice from episodic intervention to continuous protection—enabling shared agency, integrated coordination, and non-local revenue expansion.

This BOI opens new pathways for value creation and connection—grounded in the firm's existing capabilities and worldview. It turns legal strategy into life infrastructure, and creates clarity about how to inhabit that future now.

This transformation positions legal practice as essential life infrastructure rather than an episodic service provider, creating compound value through prevention, integrated care, community data, and ongoing support.

The Power of Enabling Possibility
Each example shows how reframing through enabling possibility—and activating a coherent Brand Operating Idea—transforms brand strategy into a generative framework. It allows brand and business design to move in tandem, building the capacity to meet complexity with coherence and new modes of value.

And while some of these examples are ambitious, the approach isn't reserved for big brands or seismic moves. You can do this with any brand, in any category. A BOI doesn't have to transform the market to be worth doing. Sometimes it's a bold reframing that reshapes an entire system. Other times it's a precise, practical intervention—a small, clear shift that unlocks new value.

What matters is that it frames the brand within systems, embeds it in the business, and uses futures thinking to anticipate change. Working this way means your BOI can grow, flex, and adapt as systems evolve—enabling the brand to act with greater clarity, coherence, and capacity. Whether it sparks a major leap or a modest improvement, it's doing its job when it turns meaning and function into something that moves people.

But examples are just the beginning.

Moving from inspiration to implementation requires a clear process—one that takes you from exploration to articulation, and from idea to systemic execution. The frameworks in the next chapter provide that roadmap.

repeatability is NOT ENOUGH

Some brands scale fast. A repeatable playbook, clean design system, and a message that travels can create the illusion of momentum.

Scale looks good–until the context shifts. Until markets evolve, behaviours change, or culture bends in directions the original system wasn't built for. Then what? Scaling gets you seen. But it doesn't mean you're future-proofed.

Stretching is different. Stretching is about designing systems that flex without breaking–brands that stay coherent while adapting to new inputs, roles, or realities.

Stretchable brands aren't factories; they're networks. Less like brand books, more like living logic. Think Figma or Notion–not rigid templates, but frameworks that allow users to build, remix, and extend. They don't just publish–they invite.

When brands stretch well, they don't just respond–they generate new ideas, behaviours, experiences, even new markets.

Scale assumes uniform demand. Stretch creates new value in the spaces between the brand and the world around it.

Research across McKinsey, Bain, and MIT Sloan points to a different kind of advantage: adaptive capacity. The companies that out-perform aren't just the fastest to scale–they're the ones that build for uncertainty.

Ecosystem brands–like Shopify or Discord–don't win because they scale their message. They win because they adapt their systems.

Stretch is strategic elasticity. It's what lets a brand move, adapt and rebound. Scaling is a surface play. Stretching is a structural one.

Because, if you're building a brand for the next decade, don't just ask how fast it can grow. Ask how far it can stretch.

the inhabit process

Brand strategy demands an approach fit for the complexities companies are facing. We're at the point of change, tension, and collision—yet we have the ability and the tools to design our way into better outcomes and more value for everyone. It starts with brand strategy, and it requires systems thinking, future readiness, and business design integration.

The Inhabit Brand approach offers a structured yet flexible process for building a brand strategy that creates real value for people, businesses, and society—not by declaring purpose, but by enabling possibility.

Brands ready to move beyond traditional brand strategy frameworks can use this method to influence systems—through focus, stretch, or depth. The approach inherently builds greater systems awareness, leading to stronger strategic definition and better connection to people's lives.

This chapter introduces the general process behind Inhabit Brand. It's not a detailed how-to guide, but a high-level view that moves from systems-futures exploration to systems enablement—ensuring meaning and function work together so that the brand is truly inhabitable. Complete tools, templates, and deeper applications are available through the Inhabit Brand website.

At the heart of this process sits the guiding question:

How can we enable possibility for people?

It opens up a different set of questions, and with them, different answers.

The Inhabit Process
The process is made up of three stages, moving from possibility, to enablement, to the BOI and business design. Although outlined in stages, it's best approached as a holistic, iterative process. Many excellent systems thinking and futures tools can be used to inform and deepen each stage.

1. Inhabit Possibility
This stage reframes how most brand strategy work begins. Instead of starting with internal objectives or category conventions, you start with the system—mapping the arena, where real human needs, behaviours, and dynamics unfold. The aim is to understand the deeply personal and systemic forces people are navigating.

You identify interdependencies, surface tensions, and reframe the opportunity space—not as a fixed market position, but as a possibility space rooted in meaning and function, which together define the value creation zone. Here, you expand perspective, ask new questions, and embed people and business inside systems mapping. This surfaces the interrelationships between people, business, and context.

Futures thinking plays a key role. By using drivers, signals, and scenarios, you stretch current assumptions and reveal what could be made possible—not just what already exists. This ensures strategy is built for value, complexity, and adaptive capacity.

This stage orients strategy around people and systems, widening the aperture through the arena before narrowing focus on how the brand will enable possibility for people.

2. Inhabit Enablement
Once you've defined what's possible, the next step is to determine how the brand can enable it—first within the value creation zone, then through the BOI. This is where the shift from sensing to structuring begins. You explore the conditions, capabilities, and value exchanges required to make your possibility space real. Where can it go? What does it need to do? Is it viable for the brand?

Here, Brand is approached not as a set of assets, but as a system that must function across stakeholders, culture, and channels. You begin to prototype what enablement looks like—using the Four Modes (IP, Interface, Capability, Protocol) to explore how value could be created and distributed.

This stage culminates in answering 'How can we enable possibility for people?' and shapes potential BOI definitions based on strategy definitions (possibility, enablement, outcomes).

Critically, this stage is where strategy takes shape—defining how the brand will exist.

3. Inhabit Brand
In the final stage, the work converges. You synthesise the insights and strategic logic from the first two stages into the BOI—the unifying construct that connects meaning and function across the business. It transforms the strategy of enabling possibility into a unique business operating idea.

The BOI isn't an articulation exercise—it's a systems intervention. Think of brand strategy itself as a macro intervention: testing how the BOI could come to life, what it requires, and which concept holds the strongest potential to translate strategy into reality. This becomes both an innovation-testing and business design exercise. The Four Modes of Brand Enablement and relevant scenarios are often revisited here to refine the idea.

Once established, the BOI becomes the core design layer that guides business design through the BOI canvas.

This stage is also where operational planning begins: you translate the BOI into a usable business design canvas, design participatory structures, and define how feedback, learning, and adaptation will be built into the system. The brand doesn't just express itself—it embodies itself.

Feedback Loops and Stretch Pathways
The BOI is not static. Once defined, it must be stress-tested, stretched, and iterated through feedback loops that allow the brand to adapt and regenerate value over time—through meaning, function, or both.

This can involve:

- Returning to the Possibility/Enablement loop to stretch the BOI into new markets, categories, or value definitions

- Prototyping new modes of enablement and participation

- Updating outcomes over time

- Exploring new innovation pathways or business models

The BOI is holistic in orientation—strong at the core and flexible at the edges.

What This Approach Enables: Systems-Based Brand Strategy

In the Inhabit approach, brand strategy is a systems construct. There are six practices of systems-based brand strategy, adapted from key principles of systems thinking, that describe what strong strategy must enable. They represent the systemic roles or functions that brand strategy need to fulfill to create value across meaning, behaviour, and operations.

They also serve as a test for the BOI. A strong BOI, and its application through business design, should help activate all six. They assess not just whether a strategy sounds good, but whether it works as an enabler inside a complex business system.

As discussed in the BOI chapter, the Five Balances define what strategy must hold. These Six Practices show what strategy must do.

The Six Practices of Systems-Based Brand Strategy (*Fig. 9*)	
Practice	**What it does**
Create Coherence	Ensures the brand behaves as a whole system—making all parts work together as a clear, navigable whole.
Enable Alignment	Aligns people, operations, and experiences around shared function, direction and value.
Catalyze Change	Sparks transformation by identifying high-leverage intervention points within the system both in meaning and function.
Design Participation	Creates meaningful ways for people to connect, contribute, and shape the brand system.
Evolve Meaning	Lets meaning grow over time through real-world use, interpretation, and shared context.
Generate Value	Uses feedback loops to reinforce and expand value creation across time, stakeholders, and conditions.

The Inhabit Canvas: Merging Brand and Business Design

Though not included here, the Inhabit Canvas is the practical tool that helps teams integrate brand strategy with business design. It functions much like the Business Model Canvas—but updated for coherence across business, brand, and experience.

It incorporates:

- Systems-based thinking

- Participatory mechanics

- Brand strategy, expression, and experience

The BOI sits at the centre of the canvas, ensuring meaning and function remain aligned to enabling possibility throughout the business and different expressions of it. Conceptually, it merges brand frameworks, business design, and flywheels into a single canvas for improved clarity, coherence, and utilisation. From exploration to design and implementation, it bookends the entire process in systems thinking.

Strategy as System

Inhabit Brand is not a rigid process—it's a system for sense-making, capacity-building, and value creation. It's designed to help brands operate differently in the world.

Ultimately, this model and method ensure that brand strategy can be inhabited by everyone.

The Inhabit Brand Process (*Fig. 10*)
A Three-Stage Strategic Process for Systems-Based Brand Strategy

	1. Inhabit Possibility	2 Inhabit Enablement	3. Inhabit Brand
Description	Map the systems within the arena to understand what's valuable to people. Define possibility space.	Explore possibility scenarios and define how the brand could enable it. Define the brand strategy.	Make the brand strategy operational. Build the BOI and its systems to enable it to live and evolve.
Orientation	Shift perspective by opening up the aperture.	Shift focus from possibility to enablement.	Shift the status quo through Brand as business logic.
Key Question	What is the scope of possibility, and for whom?	How can the brand create the conditions for possibility to be real, useful, and distributed?	How do we structure and embed that enabling function into the brand itself as business design logic?
Focus	Identify the arena. Understand the relationship dynamics and interdependencies between systems and their elements, as well as the human context of value. Frame the possibility spaces through which the brand can intervene.	Understand critical certainties and uncertainties, as well as conditions and capabilities. Define how the brand can enable possibilities through different modes and outline the outcomes.	Define the brand's operating idea, prototype and test BOI and develop and structure it for business design using the BOI canvas. Refine outcomes. Use Theory of Change to plan implemen- tation, partici- pation, and feedback loops.
Core Tools	Research Systems mapping Macro-drivers Arenas and spaces Reframing	Scenario prototyping Enablement modes Value exchange mapping Outcome framing	Enablement modes 5 Balances/6 Practices BOI Canvas Theory of change planning
Meta Principles	Systems Thinking: (interdependencies, feedback, constraints) Futures: (anticipation, elasticity, unknowns, scenario design) Participatory Design: (co-creation, sprints, lived experience) Value Framing: (4P bottom line: People, Planet, Profit, Purpose)		

161

Deeper is further.

When Brand lives in the system, not above the business, it has the capacity to reach across meaning, function, and outcomes to enable possibility.

what this is for

Ultimately, this work is about more than Brand. It's about how we shape the systems we live and work within—and how brands, when used well, can become a catalyst for change that is both meaningful and useful.

Brand has always been my canvas for value creation, innovation, and business design. It's imaginative, generative, and challenging. But brand strategy hasn't evolved to match the complexity of the world it operates in. Too much of it still lives in the past—in advertising, in identity, in static frameworks that no longer serve.

It was time to do this work.

This book provides a new centre of gravity for Brand: one that moves beyond purpose statements and positioning into systems thinking, futures, and business design. It is a call to evolve our thinking about Brand—to inhabit it as something we live and build through.

The question at the heart of this method is: How can we enable possibility for people? It isn't just strategic. It's personal. It's the question that got me here, and it's the one I carry forward.

Because meaning without function is meaningless.

And in our own lives, as much as in our work, we need to enable possibility for ourselves, for others, for the systems we're part of—and for the futures we hope to create.

That's what this is for.

Notes & References

4

tl;dr

I've spent years watching brand strategy drift further away from what it's supposed to do. We're still using frameworks built for a world that doesn't exist anymore—and it's costing companies millions in wasted spend and lost trust.

The core problem: brands have lost the connection between meaning and function. They either project meaning without operational depth, or deliver functionality without relevance. Meanwhile, organisations hide behind "uncertainty" when what they're actually facing is navigable complexity.

The context has shifted fundamentally. Markets don't follow old rules. Trust flows through networks, not institutions. People navigate between emerging possibilities and systemic failures. Growth now depends on participation and shared value, not just scale.

The solution isn't another positioning framework—it's a new strategic imperative: enabling possibility. This shifts brand strategy from "why do we exist?" to "how do we exist?" From story to sense-making system that builds adaptive capacity.

Inhabit Brand makes this practical through the Brand Operating Idea (BOI)—the strategic core that connects mean ng to operational reality by asking "How can we enable possibility for people?" The BOI operates through four modes: Interface, IP, Capability, and Protocol, allowing brands to function as infrastructure that guides decisions, adapts over time, and creates measurable outcomes.

What this approach delivers:

- Strategy built to be embedded in business design to ensure operational value and full potential

- A strategic core that possesses both coherence and adaptive capacity via systems thinking and futures

- An approach that ensures brands connect meaning and function to outcomes

- Stronger measure-ability of a brand's business value

- New ways to grow through navigating complexity rather than avoiding it

- Alignment across teams through shared understanding of brand's operational role

This is for leaders who know brand matters but are tired of strategies that don't translate into business results. Brand can no longer sit on the surface—it needs to operate as infrastructure that enables people to act, teams to align, and businesses to create value in ways that actually matter.

doubts, pushbacks, & but-what-abouts

Not every question fits neatly inside a chapter. Some are messy. Some are skeptical. Some show up after a keynote or in a strategy workshop, spoken sideways with a half-smile. Others are quietly wondered, but rarely voiced. These are the lingering questions—the "But what about...?" and "Isn't this just...?" moments that deserve more than a passing line.

This section answers them directly. No frameworks. No fluff. Just clarity. And with the understanding that I care deeply about meaningful and functional strategy, no matter what names you give it.

1. Do we even need brand strategy anymore, aren't we post-brand?

No—because the world isn't post-human. Brand still matters because its core role hasn't disappeared—it's evolving. Humans still need mechanisms to navigate meaning, aspiration, and identity. That's what Brand has always helped us do.

Earlier in this book, we explored why we not only need Brand now but also why we need to move beyond brand purpose.

Through a Future Lens: The Role of Brand Still Holds
Even when we scan forward—through the lens of AI, ambient interfaces, decentralized commerce, and behavioural data—Brand remains essential. It's not static; it's shapeshifting. But it's still there. Here's how it may evolve:

Brand as agentic interface: Brands may soon show up as intelligent agents—digital companions that interact, assist, and adapt in real time.

These agents won't just inform or recommend. They'll represent the brand's character, tone, and logic of interaction.

Think of how video games design NPCs (non-playable characters): each has a scripted personality, a behavioural style, and consistent response logic. Now imagine a Nike brand agent embedded in your wearable: it might hype you up pre-run, quietly track your progress mid-session, and celebrate wins in your preferred tone—calm, playful, intense.

In this world, brand design won't just be about look and feel. It will include response style, interaction pacing, tone-shifting, and ethical boundaries. Personality isn't just metaphor here—it's coded interaction protocol.

Brand as embedded logic: Whether surfaced or not, brands must exist as metadata—interpretable by machines, discoverable via signals, and permissioned by people. Brand becomes back-end code, at least in the digital realm.

As AI systems make decisions for us, brands will be selected based on the attributes they've encoded—sometimes before we consciously engage. In this context, Brand becomes machine-readable meaning—a metadata layer that matches who we are, what we need, or how we behave.

What once lived in a tagline now lives in structured data—coded into identity systems, platforms, and product ecosystems. Imagine a sustainability-forward detergent brand. Instead of pushing ads, it tags itself in ways an AI can recognize: plant-based, safe for sensitive skin, no microplastics, refillable packaging, plus aesthetic and sensory descriptors. Your AI, understanding your household's values and sensitivities, chooses it—without you lifting a finger.

Brand as filtered experience: People will encounter brands through personalized lenses or centralized systems—wearables, AI hubs, or identity operating systems. Brand presence becomes opt-in, ambient, and context-driven.

Imagine walking through a city wearing AI-enhanced glasses. Your environment is subtly personalized. You see ads, storefronts, offers, and experiences that align with your values and habits—but only the ones that match your current context. You've previously blocked fast fashion and set sustainability as a core filter, so those brands disappear from view. You're tired, so anything high-energy or demanding is muted. What remains is calm, relevant, useful.

In this future, emotional bio-data plays as much of a role as declared preferences. As tech evolves to read emotional states—stress, focus, mood—brands may begin to respond in kind. Imagine a wellness brand like Calm integrated into a smart home system. On days when your wearable senses high stress, the brand doesn't just offer a generic meditation—it nudges you with a tone-matched prompt, dims your lighting, queues a soundscape aligned to your stress markers, and delays non-essential notifications.

Brand as intellectual property: As experiences, services, and products become modular, co-created, or fabricated at home, Brand shifts to upstream code: recipes, templates, and frameworks for interaction. Trust, taste, curation, and IP coherence anchor the brand experience.

Instead of buying a coffee maker, you might download a brand-certified template and 3D-print it at home. Or personalize a wellness supplement blend based on your biometric data, using a brand's formulation engine. In these scenarios, the brand doesn't vanish—it moves upstream, becoming the source code behind an experience.

In every one of these scenarios, Brand is no longer just a message or visual identity—it's logic in action: code, context, behaviour, architecture. It's what makes the brand portable, discoverable, useful, and meaningful across environments.

Let's connect the dots:

- Brand as Agentic Interface → Interaction IP

- Brand as Experience Filter → Discoverability IP

- Brand as Embedded Logic → Identity IP

- Brand as Emotional Environment → Affective IP

- Brand as Blueprint → Product and service IP

In all these scenarios, the role of Brand becomes more ambient, embedded, and agentic—but never irrelevant. Brands still organize value. Brands still earn attention. Brand still connects identity to offer. It just does so in new places, new formats, and new conditions of trust.

2. How are brand purpose and brand enablement really different? And doesn't it have the potential to fall into the same trap as purpose?

The simplest way to express the difference is: Purpose asked: "Why do we exist?" Enablement asks: "How do we exist?"

But the real distinction runs deeper—it's about orientation and economic relationship.

Brand Purpose is brand-centric: "Here's what we believe, now align with us." It puts enormous pressure on brands to be the protagonist of social change, regardless of their actual scale or role in people's lives.

Enablement is people-centric: "What are you trying to do? How can we help?" Instead of asking people to adopt what the brand is trying to achieve, it focuses on expanding what people want to achieve.

This creates a fundamentally different economic relationship:

- Purpose creates alignment economics—people buy into your belief system and values

- Enablement creates capability economics—you invest in expanding what people can do, be, or achieve

The Brand Operating Idea (BOI) systemizes this people-first orientation, reconciling it with the business. It asks, "How do we structure our operations to consistently expand human (and business) possibility?"

Enablement creates social impact through systems, not missions. When you enable individuals to be more capable, connected, or creative, that ripples outward naturally. Social good becomes a byproduct of how the system works, not what the brand declares.

Enablement lets us treat brands as a source of innovation and logic—something that operates for the market. It's not about having a higher belief. It's about designing systems that expand possibility.

With the Brand Operating Idea (BOI), enabling possibility becomes concrete, actionable, and functional. It can't fall into the same traps as brand purpose because it's designed to solve for those historical weaknesses.

However, any model or framework can be misapplied if a business has no appetite for using it as intended or not filling the model with strong inputs and synthesis.

3. If Brand is already hard to execute, shouldn't we simplify it instead of making it more complex?

We're not adding complexity—we're designing for the complexity that already exists.

The challenge isn't that Brand is too complex, it's that most brand frameworks try to oversimplify a complex reality, creating disconnected touchpoints, conflicting messages, and siloed efforts that actually make execution harder. There's no mechanism to move from brand framework to business design.

The Brand Operating Idea (BOI) becomes a coherence engine. By informing the BOI with systems thinking, futures thinking, and innovation principles, it creates a single construct that interconnects with business model, experience design, and operations. Instead of multiple competing frameworks, you have one shared orientation of meaning and functionality. No broken telephone.

Systems only work when they're aligned on function. When everything connects through the BOI, you get clearer guidance for every decision rather than leaving people to guess how to apply brand strategy to their functional area.

This is anticipatory design, not prediction. You're not trying to predict "the future"—you're designing for multiple plausible futures and finding your space and value within them. You're actively designing toward something with intent, using complexity as a design tool rather than fighting against it.

Think of it like a tree: deep roots, flexible surface. Because the foundation is deep and coherent, the surface expressions can be more fluid and adaptive to change. The BOI creates gravity and anchor—but that stability actually enables more agility, not less.

When you embrace a systems orientation, you understand complexity and use it for design. This makes everything simpler, not more complex. You have one framework that moves with business complexity rather than breaking under it. You essentially nullify uncertainty.

The alternative—trying to keep Brand "simple" in an increasingly complex world—is what creates operational confusion and turns Brand into advertising-only. We're not making the brand more complex. We're making it more capable of handling complexity.

4. What if our organisation isn't ready for this? How do we build the shared understanding needed to implement something like BOI?

That's not only a fair question—it's the real question. Brand strategy has struggled to maintain coherence in meaning, let alone move deeper into the organisation, for decades.

Many organisations aren't structurally or culturally set up to implement brand strategy as anything more than a marketing tool. Brand is still seen by many as expression, not infrastructure. So it's not surprising when brand strategy collapses at the implementation stage. It's not a failure of intent—it's a failure of structural integration.

But this isn't a reason to retreat from strategic ambition. It's a reason to design for readiness.

The truth is: you don't build shared understanding before strategy—you build it through strategy. That's the power of co-creation, prototyping, and participatory methods. When you treat brand strategy as something to be inhabited—not just defined—you shift from delivery to involvement. The work becomes the means of alignment.

Too often, strategy is presented as a finished deck—smart, clear, static. But when a strategy is revealed instead of developed with others, it doesn't land. It lacks context. It doesn't feel owned. And without ownership or investment, there's no traction.

That's why Inhabit isn't just a model to fill in—it's a process to move through. It acts as a convergence tool, connecting diverse functions through shared questions and design logic. It doesn't assume readiness—it creates it.

Prototyping is central here. It's not about piloting full-scale change. It's about testing how the brand idea behaves in the wild: Can it guide product decisions? Inspire design? Influence hiring criteria? Reshape partnerships? When you start small, in real business conditions, you learn what holds and what breaks.

Prototypes are strategy in motion. They reveal operational constraints and cultural blockers that no deck will uncover. They show you where the gaps are—between possibility and reality, between capabilities and outcomes—and they give you something to design against.

Readiness isn't a fixed state—it's an outcome of intentional, participatory strategy work.

And here's the counterintuitive part: the more complex your organisation, the more you need a coherent organizing idea like BOI. Without it, people fill the gaps with their own logic, creating fragmentation and friction. But with it, you get a centre of gravity—one that enables distributed decisions to remain connected, even in flux.

The role of BOI is not to create one idea to control everything. It's to design one idea that enables everything. That takes process, not just positioning. It takes shared creation, not just strategic direction.

So no, most organisations aren't "ready." But they don't need to be. What they need is a pathway into readiness—a process that helps teams see brand not as an output but as a working structure.

5. If the Business Model Canvas already exists—and value propositions are central to it—why can't I just use that?

You can. And in many cases, you should. The Business Model Canvas (BMC) is one of the most valuable strategic tools we've had in decades. It brings rigour to business model design and offers a shared language across functions. But if you're trying to guide a brand—not just a business—then it has limitations you can't ignore.

The most critical limitation? It's missing the conceptual operating idea that connects value creation to human meaning and systemic behaviour.

The BMC helps you organize the business model. The BOI helps you design the BMC.

Most teams use the Value Proposition box on the canvas to articulate a mix of product benefits and customer outcomes. Useful? Absolutely. But not enough. Value propositions are often written in isolation and defined narrowly. They don't clarify how those benefits are experienced, expressed, prioritized, or built into the system as a whole. And they rarely create the connective tissue between business logic, brand experience, and cultural relevance.

They show what the company offers—but not what the brand makes possible.

That's why BOI doesn't replace the Business Model Canvas. It inhabits it. It gives it dimension. It's what ensures the business model is not only viable—but meaningful, trusted, and capable of evolving.

So yes, use the BMC. But don't stop there. If your goal is to build something people want to belong to, build with, or build on—then you need more than structure. You need something alive inside it. That's what BOI is for.

6. Why do companies profit from staying the same?

Companies don't resist change because they lack intelligence. They resist it because the current model is still working—financially, at least. Transformation is costly, slow, and disruptive. Optimization, on the other hand, is cheap, efficient, and easy to justify. Most companies default to improving what exists rather than questioning whether it should still exist at all.

This is the heart of what we might call **Easy Money Model Syndrome**: when the existing business model generates strong margins, delivers on known metrics, and gives teams a reliable playbook, the incentive to change disappears. Familiarity becomes strategy. 'Why rebuild when we can rebrand?" becomes the unspoken logic.

The syndrome tends to follow a familiar pattern. First, revenue justification: "It's generating millions, so it must be working." Then, risk aversion: "Why jeopardize a profitable model?" Finally, optimization bias: "Let's fine-tune what we have, not rethink it." Each one sounds reasonable. Together, they create powerful resistance to transformation.

But the real danger is momentum. Success creates its own gravity. A model that consistently delivers results builds credibility internally and externally. The organisation isn't moving forward; t's just spinning the same wheel faster.

That's the momentum paradox: the more successful the current model, the harder it becomes to walk away from it—even when you can see it's losing relevance.

The "if it ain't broke" mindset becomes a shield. But most models don't break overnight. They become obsolete slowly, invisibly, until they're suddenly unsalvageable. And by the time a business realizes the model has failed, the gap between its reality and the market's needs is often too wide to close.

The real mistake isn't failing to evolve after something breaks. It's failing to evolve while it still works.

Organisations over-trust financial metrics as evidence of fitness. They assume customer loyalty means alignment. They expect disruption to look familiar. But future viability rarely announces itself in familiar terms. It hides in signals, not spreadsheets.

This is where brand strategy becomes crucial—not as marketing, but as a lens for seeing business model obsolescence before it shows up in the numbers. Brand strategy, when connected to business model design, can create the starting point for envisioning something better.

7. Is the Brand Operating Idea a universal model or a Western framework?

The Brand Operating Idea (BOI) is not a Western framework—it's a systems-based model for how brands function. While this book was written with deep familiarity of North American and European brand contexts, the BOI is built to address a universal challenge: the disconnect between brand intention and operational reality.

In fact, some of the most BOI-aligned brands aren't Western at all.

Brands like M-Pesa in Kenya, Go-Jek in Indonesia, and Alibaba in China weren't designed for advertising—they were designed to function. They act as systems of daily life, enabling participation, creating infrastructure, and delivering value directly. These brands don't rely on messaging to build trust—they earn it operationally, through integration and utility.

While the BOI was developed in a Western context, it's worth noting that the U.S.—perhaps the most consumer-driven market globally—is often behind other regions in shifting toward values-led or systems-led models. Many nations are already advancing toward post-consumption frameworks, as reflected in wellbeing metrics like happiness indices.

The BOI is already in motion around the world—it simply hasn't always been named or structured as such. In emerging markets, it often shows up through infrastructure. In networked economies, it appears in brand ecosystems. In societies skeptical of traditional marketing, it shows up through proof over promotion.

So yes, the BOI works globally—but only if it's applied as a flexible strategic system, not a plug-and-play Western export. It must adapt in expression, structure, and articulation based on local dynamics.

Enablement is not a Western idea. It's a human one.

interludes & figures

Interludes

loveMARKS
yesterday's SOLUTIONS
tectonic TIMES
permission to REGRESS
the better WAY
participation ECONOMY
make it your OWN
brand is A PROMPT
repeatability is not ENOUGH

Figures

Fig. 1: The Brand Eras Timeline
Fig. 2: The Shift from Social to Generative Economics
Fig. 3: Eight Macro-Drivers Shaping the Era of Possibility
Fig. 4: Brand Futures Scenarios
Fig. 5: The Four Modes of Brand Enablement
Fig. 6: Laddering the Shift: Brand, Economy, and the Individual
Fig. 7: The Four Strategic Building Blocks
Fig. 8: The Five Balances of the Brand Operating Idea
Fig. 9: The Six Practices of Systems-Based Brand Strategy
Fig. 10: The Inhabit Brand Process Overview

references & reading

This book draws on over two decades of practice, research, and systems-informed inquiry into what brand is—and what it can become. Many of the ideas here were shaped not through academic study, but through repeated application, observation, and synthesis across business challenges, cultural shifts, and systemic pressures.

This work is influenced by the thinkers, frameworks, and studies that came before. The following references are organized by section—not as exhaustive footnotes, but as a guide to the foundations, parallels, and provocations that informed the thinking throughout *Inhabit*.

Selected references that informed the research and thinking behind this book, plus ongoing monitoring of industry publications, cultural signals, and emerging research.

"Advertising effectiveness research" - Daniel Starch (Early 20th c.)

"Affinity: Beyond Branding" - Goldfarb & Aster (2010)

"AI and Society Reports" - Pew Research (2024)

"Aided recall research" - George Gallup (Early 20th c.)

"An Introduction to Cybernetics (Law of Requisite Variety)" - W. Ross Ashby (1956)

"The Art of Gathering" - Priya Parker (2018)

"Best Global Brands Reports" - Interbrand (2022, 2023, 2024)

"Better Life Index" - OECD.org (2024)

"Blind Spot" - Gallup (2021)

"Blue Ocean Strategy" - W. Chan Kim & Renée Mauborgne (2004)

"Brand and Marketing Strategy; Marketing Management" - Philip Kotler (Various editions)

"Brand Key Framework" - Unilever (1980s)

"Business Model Generation" - Osterwalder & Pigneur (2010)

"Consumer and Cultural Trends" - JWT Intelligence (n.d.)

"Consumer Arenas" - C Space & Interbrand (2023)

"Consumer Behaviour, US Retail Behaviour Data" - PYMNTS (2024)

"Creator Economy Report" - Influencer Marketing Hub (2024)

"Cultural Mapping Reports" - ScenarioDNA (2021-2025)

"Design Science; Anticipatory Systems" - Buckminster Fuller (20th c.)

"Design Thinking; Human Centred Design" - IDEO; d.school (n.d.)

"Digital Trust / Consumer / Workforce Reports" - McKinsey & Company (2023–2024)

"Doughnut Economics" - Kate Raworth (2017)

"Eating the Big Fish" - Adam Morgan (1999)

"Emotional Branding" - Marc Gobe (2001)

"Experience & Business Models" - BCG (2023–2024)

"The Experience Economy" - Pine & Gilmore (1999)

"The Field Guide to Human-Centered Design" - IDEO.org (2015)

"The Fifth Discipline" - Peter Senge (1990)

"Fjord Trendsm2022"- Accenture Interactive (2022)

"Foresight Trends)" - Amy Webb, Future Today Institute (accessed 2025)

"From Counterculture to Cyberculture" - Fred Turner (2006)

"The Future Does Not Fit In The Containers Of The Past" - Rashad Tobac-
cowala Newsletter (accessed

2025)

"The Future of Advertising is Identity" - Es Rottschafer (2021)

"Future of Advertising Study" - Es Rottschafer (2022)

"Future of Retail Journalism" - The Atlantic (n.d.)

"Future Signals" - Nesta (2024)

"The Futures Cone" - Hancock & Bezold (1994)

"Futureproofing Next" - Sean Moffitt (n.d.)

"The Geiste Report 2025; Ecosystem Brands; Anatomy of Effectiveness;
WARC Guide to

Identity" - WARC (2025; 2023;2022; 2021)

"Gen Z & Millennial Behaviour Research" - CivicScience (2024)

"Global Influences" - Kjaer Global (n.d.)

"Global Risks Report, Future of Jobs" - World Economic Forum
(2023–2024)

"Global Workforce Survey; Future of Advertising" - Deloitte (2023; 2022)

"Governing AI for Humanity (Interim Report)" – United Nations AI Advisory Body (2023)

"Grey Swan Guild" - Grey Swan Guild (accessed 2025)

"Gross National Happiness Model" - Bhutan (1970s)

"Grow: How Ideals Power Growth and Profit" - Jim Stengel (2011)

"The Hero and the Outlaw" - Margaret Mark & Carol S. Pearson (2001)

"High Output Management" - Andy Grove (1983)

"How Brands Become Icons" - Douglas Holt (2004)

"How Brands Grow" - Byron Sharp (2010)

"The Human Paradox" - Accenture (2022)

"The Humankind Study" - Leo Burnett (2022, 2023,2024)

"Humankind" - Leo Burnett (2011)

"Idle Gaze" - Alexi Gunner (accessed 2025)

"IFTF Newsletter" - Institute for the Future (accessed 2025)

"The Image of the Future" - Fred Polak (1961;1973)

"Imagination at the Crosswalk" - Joseph Burns, INCITE Issue 02 (2025)

"The Innovator's Dilemma" - Clayton Christensen (1997)

"Integrated Marketing Communications" - American Association of Advertising Agencies (1989)

"JWT Planning; What is Brand?" - Stephen King (1970s–1980s; 1973)

"Key Climate & Sustainability Themes" - Oxford Economics (2025)

"Life Reimagined Report" - Accenture (2022)

"The Long and the Short of It" - Binet & Field (2013)

"Lovemarks" - Kevin Roberts (2004)

"Macro Drivers" - Futureproofing : Next (accessed 2025)

"Make Change" - Leyla Acaroglu (2014)

"Managing Brand Equity" - David Aaker (1991)

"Mark Ritson on creativity, brand, and the need for better strategy" - WARC (2024)

"Meaningful Brands Study" - Havas (n.d.)

"Measure What Matters" - John Doerr (2017)

"MIT Technology Review" - MIT Technology Review (accessed 2025)

"The Multiplayer Brand" - Future Commerce (2023.)

"The Multiplayer Brand; Decoding Community" - Zoe Scaman (2023)

"The Mycelium" - Tijn Tjoelker Newsletter (accessed 2025)

"The New Strategic Brand Management"; "Brand Prism" - Jean-Noël Kapferer (1992, 2012; 1992)

"The Nexialist" - Julio Estrella Newsletter (accessed 2025)

"Not Boring" - Packy McCormick (accessed 2025)

"Nudge" - Richard Thaler & Cass Sunstein (2008)

"Platform Revolution" - Parker, Van Alstyne, Choudary (2016)

"Positioning: The Battle for Your Mind" - Al Ries & Jack Trout (1981)

"The Power of Brand Ecosystems" - WARC (2024)

"The Practice of Management" - Peter Drucker (1954)

"Precision Consumer 2030" - Sparks & Honey (2019)

"Predictably Irrational" - Dan Ariely (2008)

"The Product and the Brand" - Burleigh Gardner & Sidney Levy (1955)

"Progress towards the Sustainable Development Goals: Report of the Secretary-General" - United

Nations (2023)

"Purpose vs Meaning in Brands" - Meaning Global, Dr. Martina Olbert (2023)

"Reality in Advertising" - Rosser Reeves (1961)

"Report on the Measurement of Economic Performance and Social Progress" - Stiglitz, Sen, & Fitoussi

(2009)

"The Resurrection of Retail" - Special Report, The Atlantic (2022)

"Scenario Planning Method" - Royal Dutch Shell/Pierre Wack (1970s)

"Scientific Advertising" - Claude Hopkins (1923)

"The SI Network" - Strategic Intelligence Network (accessed 2025)

"Six Pillars of Futures Studies" - Sohail Inayatullah (n.d.)

"Sociology of Business" - Ana Andjelic Newsletter (accessed 2025)

"Start With Why" - Simon Sinek (2009)

"State of AI Report" - McKinsey & Company (2023)

"Strategic Brand Management" - Kevin Lane Keller (1998)

"Strategic Foresight Reports" - Grey Swan Guild (n.d.)

"Strategyzer" - Business Model Canvas (2010)

"Systems Thinking and Disruptive Design Methoc" - The Unschool, Leyla Acaroglu (2017, 2019-2021)

"Systems Thinking Principles" - Russell Ackoff (2015)

"Systems Thinking: Managing Chaos and Complexity" - Jamshid Ghara-jedaghi (2006)

"Systems-Led Design" - Copenhagen Institute of Interaction Design (n.d.)

"Tech Trends" - Future Today Institute (2024)

"Ten Types of Innovation" - Larry Keeley et al (2013)

"Theory U" - Otto Scharmer (2007)

"Thinking in Systems" - Donella Meadows (2008)

"Thinking, Fast and Slow" - Daniel Kahneman (2011)

"The Thrive Paradox" - C Space & Interbrand (n.d.)

"Top 10 Global Consumer Trends" - Euromonitor (2023–2024)

"Trend Management Toolkit" - Anne-Lise Kjaer (2014)

"Trust Barometer" - Edelman (2022, 2023)

"Trust, Truth and The Future of Commerce" - Sparks & Honey (2019)

"The 21c Brand Economy" - IAB (2018)

"The 60 Minute Brand Strategist" - Idris Mootee (2003)

"Uncertainty: Making Sense of the World for Better, Bolder Outcomes" - Grey Swan Guild Cygnus

Publishing (2023)

"U.S. Retail and Consumer Behaviour Data" - PYMNTS (2023)

"Vibecession" - Kyla Scanlon (2022)

"Welcome to the Creative Age" - Mark Earls (2002)

"Zag; The Brand Gap" - Marty Neumeier (2003, 2007; 2005)

List of Brand Examples

- 7UP

- Airbnb

- Amazon (Alexa)

- Apple (incl. Apple Pay)

- Ben & Jerry's

- Camay (P&G)

- Campbell's

- Coca-Cola

- Collina Strada

- Discord

- Disney

- Dove

- Duolingo

- Enron

- FedEx

- General Mills

- Glossier

- GM (OnStar)

- Golf Wang

- Heinz

- H&M

- IKEA

- Lego

- LePage

- Lever Brothers

- Linux Foundation

- Liquid Death

- Lululemon

- Mike's Hard Lemonade

- Monzo

- MSCHF

- Netflix

- Nike (incl. Nike x Off-White and RTFKT / Nike Digital)

- Notion

- Patagonia

- Pears Soap

- PYMNTS

- Quaker Oats

- Raspberry Pi

- Red Bull

- Roblox (incl. Vans World)

- Ryanair

- Sandy Liang

- Shopify

- Starbucks

- Stripe

- Supreme

- Tesla

- Toyota

- Uber

- Ukraine (AI avatar example)

- Unilever

- Virgin

- Volkswagen

- Worldcom

- Zara

Note: Several hypothetical examples are used to illustrate BOI log-ic. These include composite or anonymized business scenarios across healthcare, consumer goods, and digital services. All examples, including speculative ones, were developed using the Inhabit Brand approach.

about the author

Esmé (Es) Rottschafer is a strategist, futures thinker, and founder of *Inhabit Brand*—a systems-thinking approach to brand, innovation, and business design.

She's spent over two decades working across industries and strategy roles—agency, in-house, consulting, and advisory. Her multi-disciplinary skill-set, depth of experience, and neurodivergence give her a wide and layered perspective on the interrelationships between the forces shaping our world, brand strategy, and business design.

This book is the result of a career spent inside the mess of business systems and brand strategy—written to help it evolve into something more honest, more useful, and more alive.